Wrestling
With
An
Angel

Wrestling With An Angel

FIGHTING FOR FAITH IN TIMES OF STRUGGLE

DANA HAWKINS

DPI

DISCIPLESHIP
PUBLICATIONS
INTERNATIONAL

www.dpibooks.org

Wrestling with an Angel
©2010 by DPI Books
5016 Spedale Court #331
Spring Hill, TN 37174

Printed in the United States of America

Cover Design: Brian Branch
Interior Design: Thais Gloor

ISBN: 978-1-57782-253-0

For those who are wrestling with life
and need a reason to make it through to the dawn.

CONTENTS

ACKNOWLEDGMENTS

I want to thank Sheila Jones and the DPI staff for the opportunity to write this book. I appreciate you giving me a chance for my voice to be heard in hopes that telling my story may help others to better understand theirs.

I also want to thank Echo Garrett for her heart and careful eye in helping to edit this book. I realize your life keeps you running at a rapid pace and you are constantly juggling many projects at a time. I am so grateful to you for squeezing me in.

Ben Barnett, I am forever in your debt for planting the seed that made a dream become reality for me. Your faith in me means more than you can know.

Steve Brand, you and I have traveled a long journey together. I am so thankful that God brought you into my life at just the right time. You have helped save me on so many levels. My life would not be where it is today without your grace, training and compassion.

A special thanks to my kids for your endless patience with me. Your unconditional love changes who I am each and every day. In you I have been given the best gifts in life.

And lastly, Bryan, your love has healed me in ways I can't begin to explain. You are the best of everything good, always. Traveling through this life by your side makes everything worthwhile.

Introduction

WRESTLING THROUGH THE NIGHT

Drenched in sweat, lying prone in the dirt, Jacob refused to give into his attacker. Something in him knew not to give up this battle without gaining his just reward—God's blessing. He pushed his body past the point of exhaustion, straining with all his physical energy to somehow win this seemingly impossible battle between God and man:

> That night Jacob got up and took his two wives, his two maidservants and his eleven sons and crossed the ford of the Jabbok. After he had sent them across the stream, he sent over all his possessions. So Jacob was left alone, and a man wrestled with him till daybreak. When the man saw that he could not overpower him, he touched the socket of Jacob's hip so that his hip was wrenched as he wrestled with the man. Then the man said, "Let me go, for it is daybreak."
>
> But Jacob replied, "I will not let you go unless you bless me."
>
> The man asked him, "What is your name?"
>
> "Jacob," he answered.
>
> Then the man said, "Your name will no longer be Jacob, but Israel, because you have struggled with God and with men and have overcome."
>
> Jacob said, "Please tell me your name."
>
> But he replied, "Why do you ask my name?" Then he blessed him there.

> So Jacob called the place Peniel, saying, "It is because I saw God face to face, and yet my life was spared."
>
> The sun rose above him as he passed Peniel, and he was limping because of his hip. Therefore to this day the Israelites do not eat the tendon attached to the socket of the hip, because the socket of Jacob's hip was touched near the tendon. (Genesis 32:22–32)

Jacob is on his journey, making his way to see his brother, Esau. After sending his entire family ahead of him, he is left alone and unexpectedly finds himself wrestling with a stranger, presumably an angel. The Bible doesn't say where he came from or why he is there. There doesn't appear to be any purpose other than to wrestle with Jacob, which he does for an entire night.

The wrestling is so intense that the man asks Jacob to let him go at daybreak. It is then we become aware that Jacob realized all along that he has been in the presence of God because his response is, "I will not let you go unless you bless me."

This statement indicates that he knew the man he had wrestled with was a holy man. We also learn earlier in the passage that the man was unable to overpower Jacob and therefore changed his name to "Israel" (v28) because he had "struggled with God and with man and [had] overcome."

What an honor!

Jacob consecrates the place by giving it a holy name and recognizes that "it is because I saw God face to face, and yet my life was spared" (v30).

This passage of scripture is so humbling. God comes to Jacob in the middle of the night. He doesn't explain why he's there. He wrestles him for hours, past the point of exhaustion, and cripples him in the process. He decides when the match is over and then leaves without explanation basically saying, "Good job," and Jacob has to be satisfied with that.

Also, God never really makes himself known. Jacob becomes aware on his own. He realizes during the struggle that God is the one he is wrestling with, and he is humbled at the realization that he is allowed to live after having seen God's face. No man had ever done this before.

My first instinct if I were physically in a struggle with God would be to quickly surrender, bow, fall with my face to the ground, recognizing holiness, but certainly never to fight with him. Jacob fought so hard that he made it impossible to be overpowered. Wow! Why would he do that knowing it was God? Good question. One I'll have to ask in heaven perhaps. But the very magnitude and determination of Jacob's effort got the Lord's attention.

God put his "mark" on Jacob for the rest of his life, but he spared his life after allowing him to see him face to face. Two miracles: Jacob got to physically touch God and to see God's face and live. It forever changed the kind of man he was and his legacy on earth. His battle defined him for generations to come.

The same is true for us. We may not have seen the Lord face to face, but our battles, our times of wrestling with man and with God have forever defined us and are creating our legacy here on earth.

When we wrestle with something difficult, like Jacob, we may not have seen it coming. Hard times can come without explanation or warning, and they can leave just as they came. But if we fight as hard as Jacob did, if we hold on expecting a blessing, we can have the "mark" of God on us afterwards, identifying us forever as his child.

My husband, Bryan, was a national wrestling champion in college, so this scripture holds special meaning to me. I've gotten to take a peek inside the world of wrestling and realize how taxing it can be on the body. A couple of matches will leave you with aches and pains, so an all-night match must have seemed an eternity.

It is also encouraging to have this passage as the platform for my book because I feel that in a small way it pays tribute to Bryan. He is one of the strongest people I know, so I see and understand exactly how much character is built through wrestling.

I am going to share with you many of the difficulties I have faced in life, along with those personal demons that seem to plague me on a day-to-day basis. I also want you to see how God has not only provided for me in these struggles, but has continued to rescue me again and again. I hope this book encourages you to wrestle through to the dawn and to trust that God's blessing is in store for you.

1

WRESTLING WITH DEPRESSION

In my efforts to better understand depression, I learned there is a genetic link. This led me to realize that perhaps this was a battle I had fought very early on, so I decided to go back to my beginning and work my way forward. I needed to see how the path I have walked in this life may have contributed to my daily inner struggle.

Childhood

I grew up on the south side of Chicago. My reflections on being a little girl do not include times of hopscotch, jump rope and Barbie dolls. I don't hold dear memories of family vacations with sing-alongs in the car and building sand castles on the beach. There were no game nights around the kitchen table or home videos by a cozy fire.

Chicago is an old city. The South Side was very run down and dirty even forty years ago. Families worked hard to keep their lawns well manicured and their houses maintained, but the surrounding streets were anything but well maintained. The house I grew up in was one block away from a busy street filled with stores, fast-food restaurants, loud noise and endless

traffic…Halsted. It didn't seem odd to me as an eight-
or nine-year-old to regularly cross two lanes of traffic
to get to the corner newsstand on Sunday morning to
get my dad's paper. Unaware of the traffic lights, I
would often dodge cars on my way to the candy
machines in the gas stations. Pocket money was rare
but when given that privilege, we would also run into
the local liquor store for giant bags of cheese popcorn
or Lay's sweet and sour potato chips.

Vagrants would sit outside the doors with bottles
wrapped in brown paper bags, smoking cigarettes and
passing the hours of their day. It was a normal part of
life and wasn't the least bit scary to me until the one
or two times older kids jumped me for my money or
treats, and sent me home in tears. I would race up the
wide porch steps of the house, tear open the screen
door and rattle off my trauma to the first person I
encountered, which was usually an older sibling who
would then tear around the corner in pursuit of the bullies in an effort to avenge me and retrieve my money.

Although I became more cautious in my ventures
and possibly quicker in my run back home, I never
stopped passing up and down this street. After all,
Jack-in-the-Box and Kentucky Fried Chicken were
there; Sun Drugs had the best penny candy; and Jewel
Grocery was where my friends and I frequently stole
snacks. I had a private stash in my bedroom closet that
my mother found one day. She marched me right
around the corner into the manager's face and forced
me to tell what I did, give it all back, and apologize.

Humiliation is a great deterrent.

Needless to say, my days as a petty thief came to an abrupt halt. The belt across my backside repeatedly had a little to do with that as well. I eventually learned to be really good because I saw what happened to my older siblings if you weren't. I saw my dad once "discipline" my teenage brother by taking him into the basement and having an actual fist fight with him. I remember him yelling something about "if you want to act like a man, I'm going to treat you like one." My brothers and sisters and I sat upstairs crying as we heard the beating take place.

I can recall a time when one of my sisters upset him. He grabbed her by the front of her shirt and slammed her into the wall. When I was spanked by him, I would be left with bleeding welts all over my back, buttocks, legs and arms. I was terrified of his temper, so I tried desperately to stay out of harm's way. Both my parents were very strong disciplinarians, so a punishment in our home was something to be avoided at all costs.

As I look back, I can't think of many happy times with my dad. I instead remember him drinking beer, fighting, yelling at us, or being upset with my mom, his home, his life. He was always working, so I rarely saw him unless it was a weekend. I was usually fast asleep by the time he came in at night. I imagine that despite all his hard work, he didn't feel he had much to show for it. Holiday meals were always very special, but there were certainly Christmases without presents.

There seemed to never be enough money for those kinds of extras.

Dad was not a man of many words, and that made it very hard for me as a young child to establish a strong emotional connection with him. When I got older, I asked him once how he felt about being a father. He said two things to me that I will never forget. The first was, "If I had it to do over again, I would never have had any of you," and the second was that he didn't much enjoy being a parent. I did not know how to respond to this. It left me feeling unwanted and unloved. I would spend many years afterward trying to be good enough to earn his love.

There were many opportunities to get into trouble in our neighborhood if one chose to do so. I'm not sure I understood what gangs were, outside of the talk in the school yard. Kids would taunt and brag about which of their relatives belonged to which one as a means to intimidate or manipulate. It sounded very menacing and certainly something to fear. It wasn't until it became a reality in my own family that I witnessed its horror first hand.

I can recall being told to avoid playing at the end of the block by the red house with the big fenced yard as that was a family with several gang members. The youngest of the bunch would pick fights with us just because they could. One of my scariest memories was when my oldest brother had gotten into trouble with one of the neighborhood gangs. One of the guys in the gang got into a fight in the street with him. The rest of us kids watched from the porch screaming and crying because other gang members trapped us there and wouldn't let us go get help. We watched them slam my brother's head onto the cement siding of a house. He was pounded and kicked and beaten until he was bloody, and we all stood by helplessly and did nothing. There was nothing we could have done.

There was a lot of temptation lurking about. I watched several of my siblings dabble with cigarettes, drugs, gangs and alcohol and saw the wrath that ensued when my parents found out.

We fought each other like all children do I suppose. But somehow our fights seemed to always escalate into extreme violence. The brother closest to me in age fought with me the most. As normal as that sounds, our fights were anything but normal. I remember him chasing me through the house once with a butcher knife, and as I ran through the front door, he narrowly missed stabbing me and instead slashed a hole in the screen door. He would come after me with cast iron skillets or other blunt objects in his rage. One of my older sisters got mad at me once and straddled me on the floor and beat me across my face and body until her anger was spent. When they weren't coming after me, I watched them go after each other. Anger was the prevalent emotional tone of my home.

Even playtime was something to be feared. I can recall a time when a neighbor girl wanted to beat me up, and instead of my siblings protecting me or taking my side, they forced me into the backyard and locked arms in a circle so I couldn't escape. I scanned the yard for a way out. The thin sidewalk along the metal fencing was my best bet. It was closest to the garage, and I made a run for it but they pushed me back into the center.

I tried yelling "Help," hoping one of the neighbors in either of the adjacent houses would open a door or window and rescue me. I stared in disbelief at my family when they began laughing at me and calling me a "sissy." Realizing there was no way out, I fought, hearing loud cheers of "hit her," "slap her." It took me a couple of minutes to realize the cheers were not for me, but were rather directed at my neighbor. My own siblings yelled and clapped as I took a beating. Filled with rage and hatred, I fled the yard in tears as I heard their taunts of "baby" following me.

Later that day I told my mother what had happened, and she called everyone into the dining room except me; I was excused to the kitchen. I sat quietly at the old Formica table fiddling with the salt and pepper shakers as I listened to my mother's hushed tones of rebuke and discipline. As she spoke of her shame and disappointment, I stared absently around the room at the brown refrigerator and olive green stove. I rubbed my socks up and down the cold metal of the chair legs and wondered what I had done by telling? Would I face an even worse fate for getting them all in trouble?

Home was not a safe haven. Though in later life we became closer, at that point I feared my parents and didn't like my sisters and brothers. Several times I ran away from home. I was younger than ten, so I don't imagine I went far, but I do remember roaming the streets and hiding in alleys, sitting by garbage cans for hours…or I'd try to get lucky and sneak into an open garage with a quiet corner. Garages back then were smaller buildings separate from the home, usually toward the back of the property. They were generally a place of storage for the discarded and unwanted items of a home. I would sit among the rusted bikes and cobwebs, breathing in the dank smell of mildew and just plain "oldness" with the knowledge that I'd never be discovered there, not even by the owners.

I wanted to be any place but home. I knew eventually my family would look for me, so I steered clear of all my friends' houses or any favorite play places. I would daydream and fantasize about a better place, a better life, a better family.

I learned to love my alone time. I created opportunities to be off by myself. One of my favorites was bath time. I could close the door and lose myself in my imagination for a time. I would sink beneath the bubbles in the old claw foot tub and dream the time away. The window directly above the tub faced into my neighbor's kitchen. If I stretched high enough on my tiptoes, my head would peek just far enough out, and I would call to my friends next door. They would come to their window, and we would whisper our secrets across the breezeway until we feared being caught.

I have memories of hiding in a closet or in the eaves upstairs or under a bed. These were my secret, private places where I could be invisible and feel safe. I hid from the noise, anger and violence that were in my home.

I was about nine when I began drinking beer and experimenting with cigarettes. I would sit outside on the cement porch steps of one of the brick houses that lined our street, waiting for one or more of my siblings to come out. Beer and cigarettes were my rewards for keeping silent about whatever they were up to inside.

In school I was the quiet kid in the corner who got picked on. A few times bullies in my class chased me home and beat me up.

With eight children to feed and clothe, my parents couldn't afford much, and since I was one of the youngest, most of my clothes were hand-me-downs. I would get taunted and teased on a daily basis. Kids would pull my hair and call me names until one day I finally snapped and fought back. I fought a girl so viciously that I bloodied her nose and mouth. I kicked and punched and scratched until I had no energy left. When I saw what I had done, I ran home terrified.

It was around this time that my parents divorced. The routine after the divorce was that the five older children spent weekends with my dad regularly. The three of us younger kids were not given that privilege. We were never told why; we were just left with this fragmented family and no explanation. I believe this opened the door to my longings to not only please my dad but to make him somehow want to be with me the way he wanted to be with the others.

My mother has a very kind and caring spirit about her, and sometime after the divorce, she went through a period where she let people off the street stay with us. In her effort to help, I don't believe she realized the mistake of having prostitutes and strange men in and around a home with young children.

I shrank further into myself over those months. I hated the situation, and I probably hated the men, especially since all of them at one time or another tried to approach me sexually. I never let any of them succeed, so I never told anyone. Even my sister's older boyfriends would make advances toward me. All these things added to my inability to feel secure in my own skin. I would eventually come to be controlled completely by fear.

My mother eventually moved us all to Colorado. It was as picturesque as the best postcards portray it to be. The mountains were majestic and the views breathtaking. The snow-capped peaks in winter would have avid skiers salivating. I learned to hike and camp, swim and fish. I never fully appreciated the fall season until I witnessed the aspens changing colors and the wonder of a cool, brisk morning beside a mountain stream watching deer and other woodland creatures mill about. Cooking over an open fire and sleeping beneath the stars at night are still some of my favorite things to do. But not all of my experiences there were this wonderful.

Pueblo was a small city with a very large Hispanic

population. It was a new beginning for all of us—a new city, new people, new environment. It was clear, the very first day I stepped foot off the Amtrak train, that I did not fit in. The sights, the sounds, the foods...everything was different. I didn't recognize myself in any of the things or people around me.

The biggest adjustment for me was the culture. Although I had left behind the danger of the streets of Chicago, I also left an all-black community, which was all I'd ever known. Colorado was my introduction to blatant racism and prejudice.

In both the schools I attended, I was one of maybe five or six black kids total. Now I was not only being singled out for my impoverished appearance, I was attacked daily because of the color of my skin. I was called names I didn't know existed. This brought on a whole new spectrum of insecurity for me. I didn't know how to belong. This time I fought back. I was aggressive and angry. I taunted and teased in return. I threatened and cursed. I would party and drink because I thought it made me cool and accepted. I became sexually inquisitive with boys because I longed to feel special or loved. I would have settled for liked.

I created boundaries for myself. I would do everything except intercourse. I'd drink just enough to not get drunk, experiment with only the drugs that weren't considered harsh. I did it all. On the inside however, I was incredibly lonely. There was an emptiness I just couldn't seem to fill. I tried desperately to surround myself with things, people and activity, anything to rid myself of that longing for more...more of what, I did not know.

During the summer of 1979, God intervened. He had been there all along of course; it's just that at this time he revealed himself to me in a way that I could see. I went to spend the week with my sisters on their college campus in Boulder. My sister (the one I most resemble) had made me a fake ID, reasoning that in a dark club no one would be able to tell much of a difference. I envisioned college life the way television depicted it—wild and crazy—and I was eager to take part. I knew I could get away with drinking because my mom was hundreds of miles away. I planned to meet as many guys as possible and flirt endlessly. I was excited to "pretend to be an adult" and hang out in the dorms.

That's not exactly what happened, of course. One of my older sisters had begun to study the Bible at the time and was going to a church she loved. She was also making some radical changes in her life, so when I arrived she wanted me to share in this with her. Instead of clubbing on Friday night, I was at a Bible study with her. Instead of my endless string of men on the weekend, I went to my first Christian wedding on Saturday and to church on Sunday.

I was surprised by what happened next: I loved it all. I met people who seemed to be genuinely happy without all the trappings of the world controlling them. They were warm and unpretentious. I wanted to know how they did that. I wanted that in my own life.

My sister helped by putting me in contact with the same church in my city and set it up for me to attend regularly. I immediately began to study the Bible. I spent months poring over pages of scripture, excited and refreshed about what I was learning. I drank thirstily from the water of life. It seemed I couldn't learn fast enough. I eventually became a Christian and was adopted into God's family, a home without violence and anger—one filled with security and trust, a place where love was the foundation. My life took a completely different turn from that point forward.

My current journey with God has been thirty years in the making. There have definitely been some highs and lows. I have included an appendix entitled "The Ride of Your Life," in which I compare our lives to an amusement park ride. As I share my life with you in the remainder of this book, you will have to say it's been a wild ride. In real life I hate most amusement park rides, especially roller coasters. I have an incredible fear of heights, so if you add flips and turns to that...well, I'm out.

I realize that when I have been on "scary rides" in life, I hate that as well. I don't like change, or should I say, I don't like what it takes to produce change. I like comfort and cushiness and all the padding I can get. If I could order up my life, it would be very easy and filled with lots of happy surprises and blessings raining down from heaven daily. Obviously just a fantasy life...but a girl can dream, can't she?

When I go to amusement parks, I spend the day playing all the "ground" activities and eating ridiculous concoctions of non-nutritious food. I'm the "picture taker" for the group. I hold everybody's belongings while they ride. I like to hang in the back and take it easy. It's much more fun to me to watch everyone else make fools of themselves being terrorized and then listen to it all when they come back from the rides.

Since life doesn't work this way, I've had to adapt a little...okay, a lot! The good news is: I don't regret learning to get a thicker skin in my "life rides." I am grateful for all God has taught me along the way. Because my journey has taken me on quite a few scary rides, I wanted to write this book in hopes of sharing some of my adventures with others. My desire is that having had a look at my "day in the park," it will help you overcome some of your own fears and challenges.

An Eating Disorder

One of the biggest difficulties I face is my struggle with depression. I have battled this illness my entire life, and it wasn't until the last nine years or so that I realized what was wrong with me and was able to get some help.

When I first began my discovery of depression and did some soul searching to get to its roots, I had to go backward in order to go forward. As I traced my behaviors and mindset back through the years, I realized this monster had been there all along; it just presented itself differently in my earlier stages of life. It manifested itself through an eating disorder in my teen years, transformed into rage and self-hatred when I became a young adult, and finally became full-blown clinical depression. Depression wears many faces, so it is not always easy to recognize. Since my earliest recognition or connection came when I was a teenager, I'll start there.

We often blame society and the media for today's youth being preoccupied with weight and body image. Although I'm sure that has contributed some and maybe more than it should, this isn't always the case. I was an angry young woman in high school. I internalized not only that anger, but also the fear that came with trying to handle my life.

The Bible says in James 5:13, "Is any one of you in trouble? He should pray." I didn't do this. I chose instead to rely on myself. James says,

> Submit yourselves, then, to God. Resist the devil, and he will flee from you. Come near to God and he will come near to you. (James 4:7)

Had I obeyed this scripture then, I might have avoided all that came next. I believe the root for me is that I was starved for my dad's acceptance, and it seemed the only time I got positive affirmation from him was in regard to my appearance. I saw him so infrequently that I considered any time with him a precious commodity. As much as I feared the man, I was still a child in need of her father's love. Achievements and academic success weren't praised as much by him as a thin body was.

Being thin became my obsession, my outlet for all the buried rage. I lost myself in sports, so it was very easy to hide my disorder. I ran track, and I was on the swim team. I had two practices a day, one in the morning and one in the afternoon, so I would punish myself to burn off everything I ate. I learned from other girls how to throw up and to reap the benefits of taking multiple laxatives. People don't question a small, fit body if you're an athlete. I'd starve myself privately and eat small amounts of food in front of people, especially my family, so I wouldn't give anything away. I would weigh myself frequently in secret.

I taught myself to enjoy the pangs of hunger. Hunger pangs equaled weight loss, so I focused on the "reward." I was receiving so much positive affirmation in regard to my body that I learned to equate this to personal value. If other people felt good about me, then I could somehow feel good about myself.

This skewed mentality became pervasive throughout my life. I needed to make sure everything looked good on the outside. I was an A student. I was a jock. I joined clubs at school and stayed active. I created an image that I felt was acceptable to everyone. I still needed to be the good-enough child. The only person in my life who actually questioned me in regard to this was my mom. But whenever she expressed concern about my weight, I was always prepared with an explanation or excuse.

The compliments and comments I received became an addiction. The more people told me how thin and nice I looked, the harder I pushed to stay that way. Since nothing else in my life felt good or was good, I desperately needed to keep that praise coming. If I went a few days or a couple weeks without people taking notice, my insecurities would mount, and I'd become even more obsessed. This whole ordeal became two-fold for me. I could purge the rage through sports. It was physical and hard and muscle pounding and painful. I could walk away spent and depleted, and that felt good. Also, I could set aside the reality of my difficult life if I could feel really good about something else: my body, my appearance.

This cycle went on and on well through my college years. It was there I met a man who would teach me the beauty of self love among other things.

When I first met Bryan, I was drawn to his calm nature. We built sort of a slow and steady friendship. We lived in the same dorm, so we saw each other quite frequently. We would talk for hours, about everything, about nothing. Around him I was comfortable enough to be myself. For the first time in my life I was learning to have a relationship without pretense or fear. He was and is the only person I've ever known who is completely emotionally whole. He was warm and incredibly compassionate.

I later learned he developed that part of his character while being caretaker to his grandmother the last two years of her life. A boy of ten who was cleaning up bodily fluids, helping her to and from bed, dressing her and helping to feed her. He was so devoted to her, he couldn't bring himself to go to her funeral when she died.

Having four sisters contributed to creating this beautiful heart. He was always opening doors and pulling out chairs for women. Whenever any of the girls at church were sick, he would drop off flowers and cards. His speech was peppered with lots of "ma'ams," "yes sirs," "please" and "thank you's." The perfect gentleman. It was all just a part of who he was naturally.

Because he wrestled and I ran track, we hung out together in the gym. It was good for me to learn I could have fun with a man. What a concept. We shared a lot of laughs during workouts. We even had a couple of classes together over the years, and yes, he actually carried my books. I finally felt safe with someone. The seven years prior to meeting him, God had built a bridge to my heart, but I had yet to learn that the same kind of intimacy was possible with a human being.

I can recall delving into my past with Bryan, waiting for his reaction once he realized who I really was. I expected him to back off, maybe look at me a little differently. Instead, he offered me mercy and grace...gifts I was unaccustomed to receiving except from God. I wondered who this man was, one who could learn my secrets and still love me. I never dreamed God would let me share his love for a lifetime.

He is my port in a storm. The capital at the beginning of the sentence and the period at the end. The best part of every day, still. He makes me laugh and lets me cry. He is the man who holds my hand during a therapy session, or runs a bath for me when he realizes my day has been too much.

I rarely ask for a helping hand around the house. Somehow he's just always there, washing dishes, folding laundry, bathing children. One of my favorite days is Mother's Day because I get the same gift every year, and I love it. I get the day off. That's right. I leave home for the day. I shop, I go see a movie, browse a bookstore, have my nails done…whatever my heart desires. When I return, the house is spic and span. Those "extra" chores are done as well, you know, closets organized, carpets shampooed, all things de-cluttered. It's an amazing treat. I know I didn't do anything to deserve him, but I am beyond grateful to God for this precious treasure.

Bryan now knows my struggle with self-acceptance and how I abused my body to gain affirmation. But early on in our marriage, I hid this secret. I did not trust enough in his love to let him in. At the onset of our marriage with the college years behind me, I no longer had the daily discipline of sports to hide behind, so my rage surfaced and spilled out all over him. Living intimately with someone for the first time changes you. As if married life isn't difficult enough the first year, I added this rage to the mix. I felt wholly and completely loved for the first time in my life, and this scared me. I didn't know how to handle "normal." I couldn't function in a healthy love relationship. I didn't feel comfortable with it or know how to do it.

I was used to chaos. Chaos was my normal. Pain was my familiar. Structure, order, discipline...these were all my hiding places, and they had all been taken away along with college, coaches and sports. As a result, life was very difficult for Bryan. He was now married to someone he didn't recognize. This behavior, of course, was the same depression I lived with for many long years prior; it just dressed up differently now.

Explosive anger continued to control me for several years in our marriage. We sat with other Christians and talked and prayed through each episode, trying to make things better...and they would be for a while. But I was still starving myself and participating in bulimic behaviors, my secret comfort. I had to be acceptable now that I had become so "ugly" to people. They knew and saw this abhorrent, unacceptable behavior, and it was destroying the person I loved most. I feared Bryan would decide he had had enough and would leave me.

I began to "create" reasons for him to leave. I would pick unnecessary fights and tell him to divorce me. One time I even stopped reading my Bible and going to church for a couple of months. I wouldn't listen when he tried to share Scripture or anything positive with me. Instead, I would cut him off by going into the bedroom and closing the door, rejecting and refusing his efforts to love me.

I began spending more time with friends at work and less time with friends from church. I pushed him away emotionally. I felt I needed to give him an acceptable "out," one that made sense at least to me so that it wouldn't hurt so much if he did choose to leave. I purposely became difficult to live with by being ungodly in my speech, deceitful, manipulative and argumentative in my attitude toward him so that he wouldn't put up with me anymore.

But he remained steadfast in his love for God and in his love for me. I would slowly learn that he loved me, Dana, his wife, whoever she was, good and bad, and not just that part of me that went to church. A sobering reality for me was when I realized if I turned my back on God permanently (thank heaven I didn't), he was still my partner for life. God and my husband refused to let go of me. Bryan embodied the following passage in a very real way; he showed me who God was.

> Love is patient, love is kind. It does not envy, it does not boast, It is not proud. It is not rude, it is not self-seeking, it is not easily angered, it keeps no record of wrongs. Love does not delight in evil but rejoices with the truth. It always protects, always trusts, always hopes, always perseveres. Love never fails. (1 Corinthians 13:4–8)

The winds of change blew for me when I became pregnant with our first child. I was overjoyed and amazed at this miracle God had given me. I was being given the "biggest prize" at the state fair—that giant teddy bear way in the back that sits just for show on the top shelf to entice you into the booth. I had just won it. It was so big I just knew I'd walk through the park for a week showing it off if I could. All of a sudden, those years of awful rides seemed forgotten.

This blessing forced me to think outside myself. I finally for the first time in as many years as I could remember, stopped abusing my body. I let myself gain weight normally and naturally. I ate food and lots of it, by the way. I reveled in the taste, touch and smell. I had a life to create, and I was determined that it be healthy.

God helped me, and I had a victory throughout the entire pregnancy. I gave birth to a healthy 7 lb. 11 oz. baby girl nine months later. I wish I could say my victory continued...it didn't. The minute I came home from the hospital, I once again became obsessed with getting the weight off and fell immediately into all my old behaviors—hidden, of course, from my husband and everyone who knew me.

People were shocked at how quickly the weight came off and how soon I got my figure back (I loved the praise). For me, I was off and running again in the same destructive direction for another two years—in fact until I became pregnant with my son. History repeated itself. I did great for nine months, gave birth to a healthy 8 lb. 13 oz. baby boy and jumped right back into my starvation cycle.

I lived this way until my early thirties when help and spiritual conviction from my Christian therapist helped me connect the dots of my life and figure out why I was who I was. He said I suffered some from Post Traumatic Stress Disorder (PTSD). I thought this was just something soldiers dealt with when they returned from war or people who had experienced an horrific event such as an earthquake. But he showed me that this was what I was dealing with.

As a child, I didn't have the emotional maturity to process my home life and the things I went through, so a child's mind will store those things away somewhere in the psyche so that he or she can still function day to day. It was not until my adult life became more than I could handle that those same childhood emotions of helplessness emerged. When my present-day emotions began to mirror those of the past, that little corner of my mind that held so tightly to those memories finally let go, and my past issues were now front and center. It was time to heal the past so that I could address the future. It was time for that little girl inside to finally be set free. I was given hope that I could be different and no longer enslaved to and defined by an eating disorder:

> Not only so, but we also rejoice in our sufferings, because we know that suffering produces perseverance; perseverance, character; and character, hope. And hope does not disappoint us. (Romans 5:3–5)

However, I didn't begin therapy because of the eating disorder. I went because by this time I battled severe depression. I imagine after the birth of my children, I was experiencing postpartum depression, or at least that's how it appeared to most medical doctors.

But because I had been masking real depression for decades now, it blew up, and those stages of rage transformed themselves yet again into crippling, clinical depression.

In the next section I will focus on wrestling with this stage because it is where I am today, and it is what's most real for me. No...the eating disorder didn't disappear. I have many long periods of victory now however. I can go months or even a couple of years without giving into the behaviors. My thoughts and emotions, however, are in a constant battle. There is never a day that goes by for me when I look in the mirror and feel great about what I see. I usually feel fat and feel that I look unattractive. On a "good" day, mind you, I may only think about my weight twenty to thirty times. On a bad day, I will have at least fifty or more thoughts of body weight, appearance and disfigurement.

I have put on twenty to twenty-five pounds since my days of starvation. If I'm struggling and giving in, that number can go down ten pounds. If I allow myself to focus on God, and not myself, and live conscious of what I know in my head and not what I feel in my heart, I keep all twenty-five pounds, which is probably the weight my body was designed to hold.

I'm no longer called skinny by anybody (which is a struggle for me), but I'm not considered fat either. At least that's what others tell me. I'm average in height, weight and appearance, and I have to fight every day mentally and emotionally to be okay with that description. I don't see myself through physical vision; I see myself through warped, emotional feelings. I have accepted that these feelings aren't accurate. I relate to what Jeremiah said long ago:

> The heart is deceitful above all things
>   and beyond cure.
> Who can understand it? (Jeremiah 17:9)

I certainly cannot. I'm leaving it up to God. I am determined to wrestle with it until God blesses me with a consistent victory.

Clinical Depression

The first step in dealing with clinical depression is acknowledging that it is a very real, very devastating illness. It can be life threatening when not treated properly. I cannot explain medically in detail what takes place. I do understand, however, that it stems from a chemical imbalance in the brain.

It is a strange monster. It sneaks up on you when you least expect it and seems to strangle you until you're choking. Depression takes over your life and your entire being. It becomes who you are, enveloping you so fully that there appears to be no way out. If you try to understand it, you cannot. It's a beast with no face, but with enough force and determination to literally destroy you.

It is invisible except for the devastation it leaves behind after its onslaught. You take a beating before you ever know what hit you. Your mind is battered, your nerves are raw, and your soul is left bleeding. You are left physically weak, mentally off balance, and emotionally destroyed.

Focus is something you must fight for. Each day becomes a battle that wears you out. Then there are times when you can go days, weeks or even months feeling, thinking and acting okay...even happy. And then, without warning, some small trigger is pulled, signaling a downward spiral from which you're never sure you'll recover.

You do your best to hold it together because you hate the "black" place you live when depression takes over. Yet there's a numbing quality to the whole illness that is inexplicably comforting and secure, and that's what beckons you. Going to that place where you can be left completely alone—except that it's cold and dark in there and isolated and empty. The temporary comfort of remaining hidden is also your own private dungeon—damp and dreary and not a place you want to stay for long periods of time.

Emotional Damage

God allowed me to experience firsthand how completely crippling this illness can be. Back in early 1999, I began to experience periods of utter despair. I was in a pit that seemed to have no light, air or means of escape. I thought I was without hope and found myself devoid of energy, will or desire even to perform the most basic of daily functions. I found all I wanted to do was to sleep for days on end...for weeks at a time if that had been possible. When I was asleep…nothing was real…not people, not life and certainly not pain. I didn't care to eat, dress or comb my hair. I had no concern for my own well being.

During the lowest point of my depression, I longed to be hospitalized. It was the only way I knew to completely shut off life. I thought about checking myself in, hoping to be kept for a month or more. This way I could be assured that nothing would be asked of me. No demands on my person or my body. No appointments to be kept, no phone calls to make, nothing and no one to be responsible for. I would for once, be taken care of and have the freedom and permission to just rest without guilt. It sounded like heaven.

I was almost angry that I didn't appear "sick" enough to get that opportunity. I was so tired of giving on every level that I thought I would explode if anyone asked even one more thing of me. I longed to be a child again with no adult expectations.

As a Christian, I knew suicide was a sin, but I did not want to be a part of life anymore. I also knew I'd come too far, for too long, to miss out on heaven now. I was certain I wouldn't deliberately take my own life, so I began to pray to God to let this just be the end. I reasoned that I'd fought the good fight for more than twenty years, and could I please just come home? I begged him and prayed this for months.

I remember going into my oncologist for a checkup after my second breast biopsy. I secretly hoped he would tell me I had cancer. That way I could die without having to harm myself. My life would be over, and I could finally be with God. I would also have enough time before the end to say my good-byes and try and help those I loved to become Christians.

I'd taken the time to write out my last wishes and what I wanted for my funeral. I updated my will. I wrote letters to my husband, children and those closest to me and sealed them—all prior to what I believed was going to be my visit of "good news." I was so disappointed when he said the lump, like the first one, was benign. In addition, I no longer needed my visits to him every six months (which I'd had for the past two years). My prognosis was so good, in fact, that I would not need to be seen for another three years, when I turned forty.

Disappointed and angry, I left his office in a daze. I couldn't understand God's thinking in keeping me here. Why allow me to continue to live in this nightmare that had become my life? Weren't twenty years of service enough? I was not paying attention to my driving as I questioned and pleaded with God on the way home. I turned up one street, oblivious of any other drivers, and a tractor-trailer pulled directly out in front of me. I screeched my brakes at the last minute only to look up and realize that I'd almost gone underneath the bed of the truck. This accident surely could have taken off the top of my car along with my head. Instead of this awareness sobering me, I silently berated myself for not even being able to "kill myself" correctly, even though I'd not planned the accident.

A few days later, while driving to my part-time job, I was sitting at a major intersection waiting for the light that would allow me to turn left. When the light changed, I proceeded with my turn. Once around the corner, a car was coming at me head on, in my lane, going in the wrong direction. I felt the steering wheel swerve to the right just in time to avoid the collision. Unfazed, I continued on to work irritated at the other driver for not having enough sense to be on his side of the road.

It wasn't until I was at work that what had happened began to sink in. I realized God and his angels had protected me yet again, because I was in no state of mind to protect myself. I have no memory of having turned the steering wheel and believe my angel must have done so.

Physical Aspects

I told myself I should be able to push through and tried convincing myself to snap out of it. The harder I pushed to "move on," the more my body rebelled. I'd begun to black out at random times without warning. I would walk through the house and find myself clutching banisters and furniture to keep my knees from buckling underneath me. Waves of dizziness and disorientation would overtake me. Doctors suspected that I might have a brain tumor, and they ordered tests.

The neurologist determined these episodes to be silent seizures. My brain would seize, but not my body. These were brought on by stress. I would have several episodes a day at times, and there was no medication available to prevent them from continuing. I was ordered to rest and cease driving. I fought hard for concentration just to be able to care for my children during this period.

For several months I cried daily. I was filled with unexplainable sadness. Everything that was happening in my life at the time was beyond my control, and I felt lost and completely helpless to change any of it. I was accustomed to being in control and able to fix things. During this time my dad had cancer (the first of four different kinds to come), my mom suffered a stroke, my grandmother died, Bryan's great grandfather died along with his maternal grandmother. It seemed to all come at once. I could not fix cancer, strokes and the things affecting my loved ones. I couldn't extend anyone's life span, and worst of all, I couldn't make the pain go away.

I would freeze every time the phone rang. I didn't want to hear about anyone else I loved being sick, hospitalized or dead. I didn't want to know the results of any more of my medical tests. My body had been poked and prodded with so many needles within that year. I was at the doctor's office so often that I had memorized the interior of the waiting room. I knew every detail on the furniture in my oncologist's office by heart. The nurses and staff had become all too familiar faces. There was no part of my body that was my own anymore. I had been handled, stripped, smashed into machinery, strapped to tables, stuck into tubes, and had most of my bodily fluids tested in some way or another. Privacy had become an unknown commodity.

I felt physically invaded, emotionally drained and spiritually dead. I walked around attached to heart monitors and being a pharmaceutical guinea pig. I had been cut, stitched, bruised, bloated, and left weak and sore for days on end. I faced my own immortality with the possibility of breast cancer and/or a possible brain tumor, on top of all my concern for those in both my immediate and biological families who also were in the midst of medical crises.

I spent months curled up in a fetal position. I would drop my children off at school, come home and get in bed, pull the covers over my head, and cry myself to sleep. I'd lie there for hours, not moving until it was time to shower and pick them up again. Then I'd switch into my "pretend" mode where I would stay busy trying to function for the remainder of the day because I didn't want my children to know how sick Mommy really was. I hoped I wasn't scaring them.

I tried to figure out the hows and the whys of my depression. In my pride, I wouldn't allow myself to say I had a mental illness. Weren't those for people who were serial killers, or parents who went over the edge and hurt their own children? I pride myself on being strong, funny, independent...you know...normal. Therefore, I am excluded from the other category, right? Wrong! Many people suffer from this illness without ever getting to that drastic a point. I am among them.

Something I have learned in my journey toward healing is that depression is genetically passed on. Looking back over my life, I now realize that my mother spent most of her adult life depressed. I don't think she realized that she was depressed because people did not acknowledge it as a legitimate illness forty years ago. Nor were the necessary medications available to her. I don't ever remember seeing my mother happy! As an adult, having to deal with my own demons has helped me to better understand hers.

When I was a young girl, my parents enrolled my siblings and me in a karate class. I was kicked in the head and almost lost vision in my left eye. Since that time, I have suffered from severe migraines. That injury I later learned left me predisposed to depression. The two are neurologically connected.

My nature is to be a caregiver. After twenty years of doing so both in God's church and in my family, the well had run dry. In Luke 4:13, we learn that Satan tempted Jesus time and again trying to get him to sin. After Jesus' refusal, the Bible tells us that Satan left him "until an opportune time." For me, this was an opportune time. I had resisted him for over two decades. He was content to sit back and wait. Then when he thought I was at my weakest, he hit me with blow after blow.

The reality of depression is something that doesn't go away. I live with it every day. Some days it's tucked away in the shadows, and on others it's front and center, taking control of my very existence. This world where I live, in my head, can be horrifying. It's a place

I can't escape. It's hideous, and most people can't imagine the pictures I see in a day. I don't know how to begin to describe the nightmares I run from in my own mind. It's such an ugly place to be. It's cold and dark and sickening—yet it's more a home to me than any place I know. The images and shadows that crawl along the walls of my brain are very real tormentors from Satan.

When life on the outside is pleasant or good, the sickness of depression can be held at bay. I say it's kept in the shadows because every day is a challenge for me to participate in life. Jeremiah, the "weeping prophet," describes it well:

> I am the man who has seen affliction
>   by the rod of his wrath.
> He has driven me away and made me walk
>   in darkness rather than light;
> indeed, he has turned his hand against me
>   again, and again, all day long.
> He has made my skin and my flesh grow old
>   and has broken my bones.
> He has besieged me and surrounded me
>   with bitterness and hardship.
> He has walled me in so I cannot escape;
>   he has weighed me down with chains.
> Even when I call out or cry for help,
>   he shuts out my prayer. (Lamentations 3:1–8)

This passage describes what it felt like being locked in depression and unable to reach God. At the same time you need God to get you out of the pit. If you are only depending on yourself, your relief will be short lived and temporary at best, guaranteeing your next depressive episode to be much more debilitating.

If you read through the book of Lamentations as a whole, you will see the writer fight his way to a place of strength and to an understanding of God's hand throughout this process. I love this book because its emotional context allows a mirror for my own soul while consistently bringing me back to God and clarity.

❄

In the next chapter I want to take a look at things we can focus on that can provide inspiration when in depression. For each of you, these things will differ. Finding something positive that you can believe deeply helps make things easier. Sometimes it's finding those daily blessings to remind you God is still there and sometimes it's holding on to the bigger picture...that's what helps me, and it's what I want to share with you.

2

WRESTLING TO BE HAPPY

Every day I long for heaven. For years now I have fantasized about the beauty of it and longed for the day when I will see my Father face to face. I can't imagine why anyone would rather be here on earth than be spending eternity with God. I don't understand it. I realize my thinking is backwards for some. Or maybe I'm just in sync with my brother Paul who said:

> I am torn by the two: I desire to depart and be with Christ, which is better by far; but it is more necessary for you that I remain in the body. (Philippians 1:23–24)

I realize we don't actually get to choose when we will be with our Lord, but allowing it to be real inspires me. Life is difficult on its best day, while I imagine heaven to be complete joy, without a moment's heartache or sadness ever. There will never be pain or sorrow. No nightmares or horror, no darkness, gloom or hideous shadows to fear. All is clarity, purity, freedom and peace.

Yes, then I believe I will be happy, and it won't be just for a moment or a day. I will finally be able to say I am happy for always. So while on this earth, I long for and daydream about heaven. I ask God for it. I hope for it, pray for it, wish for it and I even sometimes envy those who go home before me. I struggle with each day that God has me remain here. But then I suppose even that is part of my depressive thinking.

I view life as one big meal with heaven as the dessert. Even if the meal has some of your favorites—steak or lobster, asparagus, you name it—you still pretty much sit through it (enjoying what you can) all the while awaiting the whole reason you came to dinner in the first place: the dessert…oh yes, and it's chocolate, covered with chocolate, rich and creamy with the world's best cup of coffee, now we're in heaven!

I always eat just enough dinner to save room for dessert, which is of course the best part of the meal. The rest just whets your appetite as far as I'm concerned.

So I "tolerate" life usually because for me it's painful and difficult on a regular basis. I think about heaven daily. It's real to me. It's the ultimate vacation. I wish I could hurry it along. Of course when I vocalize this, it makes me a "horrible person" because it means I want to leave all those I love. Not true. I don't know that I can explain to anyone in my life the level of emotional pain I suffer from dealing with clinical depression. Even on my best days, it's still there…just under the surface. It never leaves. I don't see life, people, things, problems, circumstances or victories like other people do. It all gets filtered through the mind of depression.

It's like seeing sunshine, flowers, beaches, barbecues, picnics and parties all through a rainstorm. Sunday through Saturday, no matter what time of day or night, the storm never stops, so you never get to appreciate how special the beach really is. You see it, and you see everyone playing volleyball and swimming, but you kind of think they're crazy because all you see is a rainstorm. You wonder why people even bother with the effort of a barbecue; it's cloudy and cold.

Nothing feels or looks like much fun, so why bother. Don't people get it? Why are they all looking at me like I don't get it?

You want to explain to those you love what it's like to live in your world but you can't, and when you do it all just comes out angry. Your spouse and your children take this personally because for them there's just no other way to see it. In your heart, you know you love them more than life. You love them more than anyone on the planet, and it's not that you desire to leave them. You desire to leave this alien being that has become your body, your existence…this thing that has alienated you from everyone and left you feeling lost; this you want to be free from.

You long for the comfort of your Father's love and the peace of your forever home.

Heaven's Angels

For whatever reason, God has decided that I am to remain here. He tells me things very clearly and very loudly sometimes. He wants to make sure I get the point. I am forty-six years old, and we recently adopted two young children. That's right...we're insane. We are starting over in our mid-forties. We intended to just be a foster family for many years because we loved what we've been doing. Well, nine children into this, God introduced us to these two very special miracle babies. Now if anyone had told us even six months earlier that we would adopt two medically fragile children, we would have said you're nuts and would not have given it a second thought. But God snuck up on us.

I was in way over my head and the children were very deep into my heart before I knew what hit me. Let me just say this...I believe God used these babies to save me more than the other way around. He gave me a son that he knew I'd have to be very present for, front and center twenty-four hours a day. Our two birth children are teenagers now, and it would have been very easy for me to sink back into oblivion and give in to the clutches of depression and not fight to be fully present in my own life. Once you hear these babies' stories you'll see what I mean.

Elijah came to us a six-week-old foster child. He was a drug baby, and as a result, he was already on medication for high blood pressure. We found out his heart was slightly enlarged and the aortic valve had some narrowing as well. We therefore made visits to his cardiologist three times a week for the first couple of months to help get him stabilized.

As time went by, we noticed he didn't seem to function or develop like other babies. By eighteen months, we had taken him to specialists and realized he was significantly delayed in several areas. He was completely unable to speak and would scream and throw himself at us in his efforts to communicate. His body was rigid and knotted throughout his muscular structure, starting at his neck and going all the way to his calves. He was unable to recognize the simplest of everyday items such as bowl, cup, spoon or block.

The State soon provided us with three therapists who began working with us every week in our home. He was given a speech therapist, a physical therapist and an occupational therapist to help with sensory motor development. The whole family learned sign language and in turn taught him, so we could communicate better.

Elijah quickly took hold of this new way to express himself, and his tantrums stopped. We learned that he has what is known as sensory integration disorder, which will be a lifelong challenge for him. He has progressed so well that he no longer uses sign language but can actually speak. He is enrolled in a special needs school in the mornings five days a week. He still receives therapy there three times a week and is improving by leaps and bounds. God is amazing.

His heart is no better but no worse. He will always have to monitor his diet and his lifestyle. He is not allowed outside in either extreme hot or cold for fear of stroke. Aside from all of this, he is a fireball of energy. He loves "ball" sports—football, basketball and baseball. He runs everywhere. He's extremely affectionate and says hi to everyone. He's such a joy to our family. If you met him, you wouldn't think he had a care in the world. We are so blessed God chose us for him. He certainly makes life special.

His sister, Kiara, came to us at five days old as a foster child from a completely different family. They are each other's best friends now. In her early days, her challenges were very different from Elijah's. She also was a drug baby. For the first six months of her life, she lived on a breathing machine. She had apnea due to the large amount of drug use during gestation ($100-a-day crack usage).

She stopped breathing on a regular basis. We made frequent visits to the hospital when we first brought her home. It was probably the scariest thing my husband and I had ever experienced. Between caring for both babies, it's a wonder either of us were sane. Somehow God has held us together and has given us what each child needed...and made sure we had enough left over to care for our older children and each other. God's promise through Paul is indeed true: "And my God will meet all your needs according to his glorious riches in Christ Jesus" (Philippians 4:19).

Kiara has come through her own storm as well. She is five years old now and as smart as a whip. We call her our "miracle baby." There is no explanation for her still being with us outside of God. She has no physical deformities, no developmental delays, no major organ challenges and no further residue. To think: that much "crack" in utero, and she came out alive first of all, fought to be here for six months, and now is a beautiful, healthy baby girl that most would never imagine had such a rough start in life.

I'm overwhelmed to say the least. But I can't imagine not being their mom. They push me to dig deep every day to find the best parts of who I am and give some of that to them. God wants me to find the best parts of who I am to remind me of what David says in Psalm 139:13–14:

> For you created my inmost being;
>   you knit me together in my mother's womb.
> I praise you because I am fearfully and
>   wonderfully made.

God wants me to know that there is good in me that he can use and that he is using every day. Depressive thinking tries to trick me into believing otherwise. The weeping prophet I quoted earlier also looked to God for perspective. He too knew that God had great plans for our lives:

> "For I know the plans I have for you," declares
> the LORD, "plans to prosper you and not to harm

you, plans to give you hope and a future."
(Jeremiah 29:11)

God has plans that stretch all the way to the end of my life. Even if I had quit dreaming for myself, God hadn't! I didn't see what else I'd be doing or where else I'd be going in my life, but God already had it all mapped out. I get frustrated and mentally quit if I can't see where I'm going or how it's all going to work out or even if it's something I'm going to want to do! That's why God didn't let me see this path of adoption until it was time to do it. He engaged my heart first because he was sure my mind would follow.

It's hard to say "no" to the beautiful innocence of a baby, especially when he or she has been dealt an incredibly unfair and difficult hand in life. And all God asks of me is to share my life with them and a little bit of love to balance out the scales. Something I've learned is that love is free! It costs you nothing. You can give it all away and you'll get more. You'll never run out. It's impossible. God will always keep filling your cup.

So I see this stage two in my life as God fighting to keep me engaged in the battle. That's not at all to say I've given up on my two older children. I see their need for me as less, the more mature they grow. They are these amazing young adults. Once high school hits, the reality of the real world comes with it. They are preparing for college, working jobs and saving up for cars. It's a little mind blowing to see these miniature adults preparing to set off on this separate journey of their own that leaves you behind. There's nothing you can do about it except love them and let it happen. You pray you've done your job as a parent to prepare them, but if you're anything like me, you're never ready to see them go. My role in their lives has forever changed. It's still there; it's just different.

For someone who battles depression, the mind is a tricky thing, and I'm grateful God is fighting for me because I don't know that I'd fight hard enough to find purpose for myself. This is when succumbing to the emotional war becomes easier. The abyss is calling. Lay back and relax. If someone's not fighting for you, it can seem like too much effort. Pray as I have: "God, help!" I didn't know what I meant or how I wanted him to help me. But thank the Lord that he knew and that he had a plan.

So for now, I am taking it one day at a time because if I look too far into the future, it scares me. I panic a little thinking "what have we gotten ourselves into?" Apparently God knows precisely the answers to that, so if I stay close to him, he will help me not to get lost.

Struggling with God

One recent challenge with depression came to me as we entered this adoption process. Something that is meant to be beautiful and special began to turn into a horrifying nightmare. Rather than turn to God in faith and patience as did my husband, I panicked and became crippled with fear and depression. I allowed anger and bitterness to take root and lead me on a journey that I could not easily break free from.

We began the summer of 2006 filled with excitement as the adoption of our son, Elijah, was finally taking place. I remember sitting in the room before the judge, signing the last of the official documentation that would make him permanently ours. We received many congratulations and hugs, and our three-year journey was finally over. I looked at the paper with his new name on it...ELIJAH JOSEPH HAWKINS, and a rush of gratitude swept through my body for this little boy that we loved so deeply. He was finally a Hawkins! In that same thought, I was anxious about the little girl at home who had lived with us for the past two years who was now awaiting her day in court. This was fast approaching. We were only a few weeks away now. A small knot formed in my stomach because I wasn't sure her adoption process would go as smoothly.

A few short weeks later, I was to appear in court again on behalf of adopting her. This time the situation was fraught with anxiety, doubt, fear and the unknown. I was not walking into a "sure thing." Kiara's maternal great aunt from out of state was also coming to court in hopes that the judge would choose her home for permanent placement. What's more, she had all of the approved paperwork and documentation from her state's Department of Children and Families, showing that her home was fit as were she and her husband as guardians for this child.

The State's policy usually is to place a foster child with a birth relative. So this game changer meant that the odds were incredibly stacked against us. Basically, if the judge ruled in her favor, we would have to turn this child, who had lived with us for the past two years, over to a stranger as far as Kiara was concerned and send her to live in another state in another home. The thought was devastating.

Kiara's attorney was there to ask the judge to have her removed completely from state custody and given to us permanently, rather than to the birth relative! Unheard of! Judges don't remove children from the Department of Children and Family and give them permanently to a foster family. The attorney was asking for two gigantic miracles. If God granted this, we faced the possibility of the State retaliating by suing us. We would be on our own financially in adopting her, an enormous burden we could not afford.

The normal protocol for adoption with a foster family is that should you choose to keep the child in your care, the adoption is free of charge. This is what took place with Elijah. Because he is a special needs child, and Kiara had medical challenges as well, the State was very generous with its financial assistance. Although Bryan has continued to work, we had become accustomed to the extra support to meet the needs of our steadily growing family, especially since I had not worked outside the home in several years. After adoption, the State will then give the family a much smaller stipend as a thank you for taking a child out of the system. You receive this money until the child turns eighteen. For those of you with medically fragile children, you know the burden can be enormous. Relying solely on Bryan's income to care for a family of six with the additional burden of litigation was not within the parameters of our reality. This was going to be a tremendous adjustment. The only other option for us with Kiara was putting her back into "the system"—no real option. We would fight for this child.

Well, God "parted the Red Sea" for us. The judge didn't accept the aunt's approved paperwork. He set it aside, stating she had not met her responsibilities to the child in other areas, so her state's approval was overturned. We didn't have to give the baby to her. Amen! In addition, the impossible happened: The judge also decided the State had failed the child, and he gave Bryan and me permanent custody, taking her away from the State. He gave us four months to get her adoption going and to appear before him again.

I was in awe of what God had done for us. I went out into the hall to speak with the baby's attorney to understand in plain English what all of this meant. The aunt was waiting for me with fire in her eyes. She informed me that she and her sister would be suing us and stormed off to begin filing papers. One of the state social workers informed me over the next ten minutes that all of our monthly financial assistance, adoption assistance, clothing allowance, gas allowance, medical insurance and any state support we'd been receiving had been immediately pulled. By 5:00 PM that day, we would have nothing. It was 4:45. They threatened me and accused me of "stealing" a child from a blood relative.

The State had been publicly berated by a judge for not adequately doing its job, and as far as they were concerned, we were somehow at fault. This was a decision that was rarely made, if ever, by a court. Our miracle was their defeat, and the intention was to now make us pay.

By the next morning, Bryan and I contacted our attorney to fill him in on everything and to find out how much we would need to adopt Kiara. He told us around $5,000. Not only had our household income been cut drastically, we needed to now come up with $5,000 in four months to keep this child in our home. Of course we began to beg God. At this point, I still had faith. I still believed God would come through for us. I reasoned that God would not give us these children and then leave us with no way to care for them. I clung to what the psalmist said in Psalm 37:25:

> I was young and now I am old,
>   yet I have never seen the righteous forsaken
> or their children begging bread.

Several weeks went by, and we had not a dime toward attorney's fees, and things were looking pretty dismal at home. I was becoming discouraged and trying not to give way to panic. About six weeks later, we were in danger of having our utilities turned off. There was no money in the bank, no food and still not a dollar toward Kiara's adoption. Bryan was prayerful and faithful. I was mad and sinful. I was angry at God for not rescuing us and for letting it get this bad. Where was he anyway? I was becoming vile in my heart. Some of our Christian friends knew of our plight and kept our utilities on, helped us with food, and tried to keep us encouraged and prayerful.

The weather here in Atlanta began to change, and neither of the babies had winter clothing or coats, and both were down to one pair of shoes. At this point, I became truly wicked in my heart and had the audacity to speak to God with venom. I share this because I want to show that when you get lost in depression and anger, it gets pretty disgusting. I want to be honest and not dress it up no matter how embarrassing it may be to me. I was so far gone I did not think I could find my way back. Thankfully, God loved me through it and people helped me. I remember telling God: "You're kidding right! Is this some kind of sick joke? Do you even see what's happening to us down here? Hello...children hungry and cold! If you could fit us into your busy schedule, maybe you wouldn't mind helping us out...just a little?!"

Then I refused to speak to him at all for two weeks or read my Bible. I figured, why bother. If he's not going to lift a finger to help me, I'll just do it myself. A good friend of mine came through with the money for the lawyer and said to just pay her back later when we were able. I had decided, "You need to get started; time's a wasting." We began literally begging from neighbors, friends and family for donations. People who could were happy to help. Benevolence at our church pitched in to keep the household running.

I felt so desperate I stopped listening to my husband. Not because I was mad at him or didn't love him. I explained that. He wanted me to wait on God...to trust, and I couldn't do that. I couldn't just watch the family sink and suffer. I felt that if we were going to survive, I had to be the one to make it happen. Bryan was already working full-time, in school for his MBA, and interviewing for a new job. He could do no more. I felt trusting God was not an option for me. He apparently was taking a nap as far as our family's needs were concerned.

I got out the Yellow Pages and looked under "charitable organizations" and found one nearby. One morning while the others were at school and work, I took Kiara and we stood in line at a homeless shelter, waiting to receive food and clothing. I was truly at one of the darkest points in my life. I thought of this passage in which Job poured out his despair to God:

> "For sighing comes to me instead of food;
> My groans pour out like water.
> What I feared has come upon me;
> What I dreaded has happened to me.
> I have no peace, no quietness;
> I have no rest, but only turmoil." (Job 3:24–26)

I believe this experience did more to change my heart than anything had so far. As Kiara and I sat against the wall of the dilapidated old trailer awaiting our turn, I looked around and saw that desperation wears many faces—sorrow, pain, need, hunger, home-lessness, hurt...theirs and mine! We feel the same on the inside; we just look a little different on the outside.

I stared into the face of helplessness, of hopeless-ness, of sadness and fear, and I saw a mirror—reflec-tions of myself looking back at me. Throughout the room so many faces were scanning the floor—either from shame of having to be in this situation, heartache from life's circumstances, or burdens too heavy to carry any further that have permanently left their shoulders slumped. Eyes downcast because there was no reason to look up, nothing to look forward to. All trying to find the mental strength to stand up again, to put one foot in front of the other.

This is not the jovial atmosphere of a doctor's wait-ing room where a neighbor visits with the person in the chair next to them. This is the somber muttering of numbers being called and information being taken. Metal chairs being scraped across the floors and noisy heaters rattling overhead. Stale air mixed with body odor and dirt. Young and old, Hispanic, black and white. Clean people and those who could not help their hygiene. There were quiet children and crying babies. Children playing contentedly with ragged toys and those hugging beloved and cherished teddy bears. Hushed whispers and stolen glances pass between us as we each in our own way wonder about the other's situ-ation. We wait for our number to be called. Pleasantries and smiles are absent. It's hard to imagine Jesus in this world, this reality...but he too was homeless: "Foxes have holes and birds of the air have nests, but the Son of Man has no place to lay his head" (Luke 9:58).

I was sobered when I thought of how Jesus would have viewed this situation, how he would have felt about this group of people and the desperation in their lives. As much as I tried to be mad at God, he crept in there and began to soften my heart. I had come for food and clothing, but God had brought me there to restore my soul. I needed to stare into his face again and remember: God has not forgotten me. Nor has he forgotten anyone else in this room. This place where we all are in our lives, it's not forever...it's just right now. It was as if God had done for me what he did for Elisha's servant in 2 Kings 6:17, when his lack of faith kept him from seeing God's protection:

> And Elisha prayed, "O LORD, open his eyes so that he may see." Then the LORD opened the servant's eyes, and he looked and saw the hills full of horses and chariots of fire all around Elisha.

That was a beginning for me. Before this experience, I was so full of rage that I could barely function. My good friend Jamie pointed out to me that I was so full of anger that I was not calm enough to hear God's Spirit trying to speak to me. That was convicting. I felt like there was a poison permeating my heart.

I had spent the past two months feeling abandoned by God. I felt hopeless and afraid. I didn't see a way out. We were living hand to mouth. I was constantly crying, walking around in pajamas for days at a time, and I didn't understand how Bryan could remain so constant in his belief that God was providing and would continue to. He'd quote all these positive scriptures, while the only ones I could seem to relate to were ones such as Lamentations 3:17–18:

> I have been deprived of peace;
> I have forgotten what prosperity is.
> So I say, "My splendor is gone
> and all that I had hoped from the LORD."

These passages were a mirror to my soul. They read my pain and identified with where I was. My mind was so clouded with the struggle of the day-to-day circumstances that I couldn't see how God had been at work in amazing ways already. A good friend of mine, Michelle Ward, told me that since I saw God part my Red Sea in court, I was like the Israelites. Now I'm on the other side, and all I'm doing is complaining about the manna in the desert and how "good" I think I had it before. I was still demanding another "big miracle" to prove his love.

So true! I don't want "manna"—just enough for each day. I want God to get us out of this now and let it all be over. Instead, he gave us a gift through a neighbor who is a Wal-Mart manager. He brought over boxes of clothes to my kids, all brand new...for both the babies and the older ones. They all ended up with so many that the closets and dressers were stuffed.

He gave us friends who love us and who would

"magically" leave care packages on our doorstep full of food and supplies. We've been getting lots of "surprise" checks in the mail. I looked down into my purse one Sunday at church and a mysterious chunk of bills was lying next to my wallet.

People offered our teenagers odd jobs on the weekends to help them with their needs. We began getting spiritual books in the mail and at church to help us with quiet times. *Falling in Love with God Again* by Andrew Giambarba was so helpful to me that I'm going through it for the third time. It literally turned me around and got me back on track. God is providing!

The one right thing I did do through all of this was to remain open with people. Even when I felt hideous to God, I made sure those closest to me knew how I was doing. I told them I was depressed and angry. I let them know I had stopped praying and reading my Bible and why. As long as someone was aware of the condition of my heart, they were able to redirect me to God. When I did begin to pray again, I began praying for others first, and I would also ask God to please hear and answer all the prayers that were coming to him on behalf of our family.

One night, my friend Jamie prayed with me, for me and about me, and that was a huge turning point in my depression. I couldn't forgive myself for how I'd spoken to God and treated him. I needed someone to go to God on my behalf and intercede for me. James 5:16 says the prayers of the righteous are "powerful and effective." I knew that having a godly woman go to

God on my behalf would help me. In my head I believed the Bible; I believed that God forgave me when I repented, but my heart needed to bond with my Lord, and for that, I needed my sister in Christ. I was so grateful to have her help to rescue me from the clutches of Satan.

With much help I was able to move past these difficulties and was hoping I would respond more righteously with whatever challenge came next. It was not long before we would find out. Shortly afterwards, Katrina literally destroyed the city of New Orleans. My family and I sat with the rest of the world horrified and sick not only from watching the tragedy unfold, but because of the possibility that Bryan may have lost all of his relatives at once. His mother, grandparents, aunts, uncles, nieces, nephews, cousins…everybody he holds dear lives in that city.

The first two weeks were traumatizing because all the phone lines were buried under water, and we had absolutely no means of communication. We watched, waited and prayed feverishly for everyone's safety. We were glued to the television, watching the grizzly images of horror, hoping not to see anyone we recognized. We waited to see if we would receive the news that his relatives were among the dead. It was literally the heartache felt around the world. I felt helpless and afraid, unsure of how to comfort my husband. The unknown was entirely too large this time.

Although I felt panic and doubt, I watched my husband get on his knees again and again. He pored over his Bible searching, somehow knowing the answers he sought were in there. He refused to let himself fall apart. We called all of the FEMA and Red Cross numbers. We called all of the hotlines for shelters, but none of the family showed up.

Finally, at the end of two weeks, we received a very staticy call from his mother saying that she and over thirty family members were safe in a church shelter in Texas. By the end of the third week, we heard from the rest of his relatives, all alive and unharmed. God had done more than we could have asked or imagined.

As much as Bryan wanted to go to them, he could not. They were letting no one into the city. It was almost a full month before residents were even allowed to go back home. As it turns out, it was even more months before he was able to get home, but I watched him cling to the cross like never before. God gave us many ways to serve them from afar. Churches from around the globe sent us donation upon donation to give. Family members and friends helped us get food, clothing and toiletries to them. For many weeks afterward help continued to pour in. His relatives were overwhelmed that complete strangers would come so immediately to their rescue. To this day, we receive thanks with tears over the amount of love they received.

I learned quite a bit as well. This time I didn't rage at God or even ask why. I followed my husband's example, and along with our oldest children we committed ourselves to prayer and holding to the promises of the Word. Somehow I remained relatively calm and focused. I had to in order to be a source of strength for Bryan. I managed to take care of all the details necessary in a crisis that he could not think of because his heart and mind were much too clouded. It was my turn to be there for him.

Remarkably, I did not fall into depression. God helped my thinking to remain unclouded by the intensity of emotion surrounding the situation. He navigated our family through the toughest of storms and helped us remain close to each other while growing closer to him.

Making it from one day to the next is still a challenge. But what is better is that I'm fighting to stay focused on God. I'm still in therapy. Depression will be a lifelong illness for me. But I cannot afford to let Satan take me out with it. I'm so grateful for friends and family that show me mercy and love me in my struggle to be well.

Longing to Be Well

I find encouragement in God's promise that there is a way out (1 Corinthians 10:13). It's not always an easy way or a quick way, but we can get out. In 1 Kings 19:1–18 we get a glimpse of Elijah as he faced depression:

> He came to a broom tree, sat down under it and prayed that he might die. "I have had enough, LORD," he said. "Take my life; I am no better than my ancestors." Then he lay down under the tree and fell asleep. (vv4b–5)

Elijah had just come off a tremendous victory defeating the prophets of Baal. At first glance, it can appear that he became fearful and faithless over Jezebel's threats. I don't believe this to be so. He, in fact, had just spent a tremendous amount of emotional energy as well as faith to obtain that victory for God, and he was drained. He had traveled a day's journey in the *desert*, no less, before he uttered the above statement to God. He was tired of giving and having to be strong. And he momentarily succumbed to exhaustion.

This became an opportunity for Satan...a trigger if you will. Once the devil was convinced that Elijah was completely discouraged (after all, it was he who put the defeatist attitude within his heart), he attacked. And Elijah gave in. All he wanted to do was eat and sleep and be left alone. God realized his state and restored him by meeting his emotional needs.

In verse 3, Elijah became withdrawn and didn't want to be around people. So much so, that he left his servant an entire day's journey behind. He hit a wall and he just prayed to die. He tells God, "I've had enough." At that point in his life he couldn't face even one more difficult thing. He became emotional, which caused him to lose sight of God's plan and to become faithless. He irrationally decided he had made zero progress and everything he had done and gone through had been for naught. He lamented, "I am no better than my ancestors."

Elijah allowed this one incident to get him to lose perspective, and he shut down. He ends up spending an entire day sleeping...sound familiar? He couldn't motivate himself to do anything more. It took the prodding of an angel of the Lord for him to continue with God's purpose. In verses 11–21, we see God comforting and humbling him. He then gave him some emotional support in the form of Elisha!

Job is another man who faces a prolonged battle with depression. In chapter 1, verse 8, we learn that there is no one else on the face of the earth like him, according to God. Not just in his "church," city or even country...God says no one on earth, period! His initial reaction in verse 20 after receiving the most devastating news of his life was to worship the Lord: "At this, Job got up and tore his robe and shaved his head. Then he fell to the ground in worship."

In chapter 2, verse 10, as Job spoke to his wife, he assumed this trouble had come directly from God: "He replied, 'You are talking like a foolish woman. Shall we accept good from God, and not trouble?'"

We know this was Satan's doing, but Job has reasoned to himself that this must all be part of God's plan for him and he wanted to accept it willingly. By chapter 3, the reality and pain of what he had been through set in, and he became depressed. He could not seem to comprehend his loss or grapple with the pain. Imagine if you'd just lost your home, all of your children, your health, and now you lose your wife's spiritual support. Devastation is putting it mildly.

As the book goes on, we see his friends are of no

help to him, and he must suffer alone as well as find a way to remain focused on God. In chapter 38, God speaks and reminds Job that he is aware and involved in all that is happening to him. He rescues him from the clutches of Satan and rains down blessings from heaven.

These biblical stories, as well as several other resources and thoughts, are helping me to get on the road to recovery. I am sharing them with you in hopes that you too will find encouragement. The following are a few things I find to be crucial to the healing process.

Trust

Learn to trust others during the worst of the pain. Fear and anxiety are usually in control at the depths of depression. So even hearing the word "trust" is scary. However, it's essential because at that point, you're not able to think clearly.

Relationships

Pick one or two people who know you very well. They will be more objective about what you can handle and when. The woman who knows me best isn't even in the same city. Kim Campbell and I go back twenty years. I trust her with everything I am. With her, I am completely vulnerable, without fear. She is my closest friend. She's that girlfriend who knows all your secrets; the one you easily laugh with and cry when you need to. She is that shoulder to lean on any time of day or night. Her well of faith runs deep, and I draw from it often. She is a woman whose life is more than worthy of imitation and whose love for me is all encompassing. Over the years we have spent count- less hours on the phone and face to face. She has lis- tened to the worst of it and rejoiced with me in the best of it. Somehow she is always able to direct me back to God and keep my feet on the ground.

Also, I implicitly trust my husband with all facets of me. There are large parts of this that he does not relate to or understand, but he loves me unconditionally… always. My security in that keeps me from building walls.

Prayer

There were many times I was so paralyzed emo- tionally that I could not even focus enough to read my Bible. At first, I beat myself up about being "in sin" and "unspiritual" for not having a quiet time with God on a certain day. But then I came to accept that there are times I just *can't*! My mind will not allow me to con- centrate. In those moments, I pray. I find I can usually talk to God. Sometimes all I can manage are a few sen- tences attached to an amen! Other times I can spend several moments or hours with God. When I find I can do neither, I ask someone to pray with me and for me. Usually my husband or a close friend. At times, I've even had one of my children pray with me about our day or something special on their hearts. I just know God hears any and all prayer. And of course with God I'm as real as I can be.

A Committed Heart

In Revelation 2:4-5, the Scripture teaches that we must remember the things we did at first—our first love for God. I was happy and eager to please him and to show him my heart. I was intent on giving him my best in the beginning. His love mattered most to me. As life has seasoned me, my affection for him has at times grown stale, and I have allowed myself to feel "status quo" is acceptable. It can never be because when I allow that to happen, it changes the whole dynamic of my relationship with him.

Depression can never be an excuse I allow myself to hide behind. It can be very easy to rationalize that "God understands I'm sick and can't do what everyone else does." That kind of thinking only opens the door to a lukewarm heart.

Although my ability to engage outwardly in deeds may differ during the rough times, my heart must always be aflame with the fires of first love when it comes to giving to my Lord. He doesn't all of a sudden deserve second best because I am struggling or in pain. That initial passion must sustain itself over the years, or my connection with him will become stagnate. If I stop making him a priority, my foundation is at risk of crumbling. Complacency with him must never become our normal.

Exercise

Whether it be walking, biking, swimming or going to a gym, find something that will give you an outlet to relieve some of the stress. I love swimming, so I go to my local gym to do laps. It feels great to just "turn off" life for a little bit. When I work out on the machines, I put my iPod on and let the music and my muscles relax away the worries. Decide what works for you and go for it.

Going Outdoors

It helps me to be where I feel God is! Away—not surrounded by buildings and traffic and people. I have a place I go here in Georgia called Red Top Mountain. I hike the trails, and I talk out loud to God. I sing to him, I cry with him, and I allow him to befriend me. This mountain is surrounded by water, and one of my favorite trails ends at a cleft of rocks, jutting out over the lake. I hike to the end and sit at the water's edge. I take in the serenity and beauty of my surroundings. I listen to birds in the distance while water dances against the rocks. I wave to the occasional passersby. I look into the sky above, close my eyes and appreciate the breeze across my face. I allow myself to feel kissed by God. Out there, surrounded by mountain, trees, rock and water…God is very real to me and I know he cares.

Therapy

Help came for me in the form of a therapist named Steve Brand. My husband came with me in the beginning because I was so fragile emotionally. The thought of going to a stranger and exposing raw pain alone was simply terrifying to me. God has taken excellent care of me through this man. He is so like Jesus in his compassion and grace. Those things went a long way to soften the hard protective shell I had built around my heart. He has helped me to not only work through my present pain, but also to look back over the years and find the root of what led up to my initial collapse in the first place. We have broken a lot of chains together and freed my heart and spirit so that when I face future storms (and I certainly will), I will be able to experience victory much sooner.

Medication

I also began taking antidepressants, which help lift the fog that clouds my mind. This enables me to think more clearly and to respond more calmly. I am able to sort things through to resolve, while maintaining my spiritual focus.

Truth

Hebrews 6:10 – There were a couple of things Steve shared with me that completely changed the direction of the course I was on. One was Hebrews 6:10, which says,

> God is not unjust; he will not forget your work and the love you have shown him as you have helped his people and continue to help them.

I needed to know that it was okay to spend time just getting well. Satan saw this as an "opportune" time to tempt me to feel guilt over my lack of impact as a disciple of Jesus. This scripture helped me see things from God's perspective. Steve reminds me of all the ways God has used my life over the years. He had a different plan for me now, which included getting well. That was so comforting to know. It allowed me to feel peace.

Luke 22:31–32 – The second passage I found to be of great inspiration is where Jesus is speaking to Peter before he denied him in the garden:

> "Simon, Simon, Satan has asked to sift you as wheat. But I have prayed for you, Simon, that your faith may not fail. And when you have turned back, strengthen your brothers."

I recall Steve making the parallel for me. He walked back with me through my life and shared how Satan was sifting me as wheat. His encouragement to me then was that my faith would not fail, as he believed it wouldn't, so I too could come back around and strengthen my brothers and sisters.

From that point forward, I have paid close attention to the things God has taught me both in life and in my times with him. I began sharing very openly with those I saw hurting and fighting similar battles to my own. I prayed fervently for them and asked for the same in return.

John 8:32 – Jesus says,

> "Then you will know the truth, and the truth will set you free."

One thing I have learned from this scripture is that the truth that brings freedom isn't always God's word. Sometimes, it's the truth about our past, our families and ourselves that we must be willing to face. And in the facing, we are set free.

God has brought me to a place in my faith and relationship with him that I didn't think was possible. My marriage continues to grow stronger each year. During the toughest of times, my husband and I cling to each other, rather than drift apart. I have borrowed Bryan's faith again and again when I didn't have enough of my own. His prayers on my behalf bring me to the foot of the cross and help keep me there as God works in my heart. God has changed the dynamic in our home. I'm learning that surrendering to my husband will help me to be at peace in surrendering to God.

I hold on to Paul's promise as I move ahead in my life:

> And God is faithful; he will not let you be tempted beyond what you can bear. But when you are tempted, he will also provide a way out so that you can stand up under it. (1 Corinthians 10:13)

I am encouraged by the changes God is bringing in my road to recovery. I am refreshed and thankful. As for what lies ahead...I am learning to take one day at a time and not to worry about tomorrow, "for tomorrow will worry about itself. Each day has enough trouble of its own" (Matthew 6:34). As I allow God to be in control of each day, I feel calmer and more secure.

Helping a Depressed Person

I have spoken in this chapter primarily from the perspective of someone who lives with depression. I realize, however, there are some of you to whom these things seem completely foreign. But you might have someone in your life for whom my experiences are their everyday reality. You love them and want to help. Because I'm not a therapist, I cannot tell you what will work from a professional standpoint, but I can offer some thoughts that I believe are very helpful as you are a support to someone else. They are gifts that people have given me over the years, and I cannot tell you what a tremendous difference they have made.

- Listen to what the person is going through without judging or fixing them. Sometimes we just need to be heard. It's okay if you're unable to relate. Just be there to love them. Sometimes that's what helps the most.
- Offer comfort and encouragement in a manner they are able to receive. Not all people are comforted in the same way.
- Give cards, phone calls, and/or thoughtful surprises to remind the person how much they are loved.
- Pray with and for them.
- Acknowledge that what they are experiencing is very real.
- Offer scriptures or books that you think may be a support to them. Don't take offense if they are not receptive yet, and don't hold them account-

able to read them. That just puts more responsibility and burden on them.

- Offer ways to serve that may lighten their load or make their day easier. Examples: make a meal, offer to babysit or help with errands.
- Arrange to spend "fun" time together, getting them out of the house and away from their regular environment.
- When you communicate, be careful that your tone and expression is one of mercy and compassion, and not impatience or condescension.
- Extend affection if they are receptive to it. Not everyone is.
- Do not tell them they're just in a "bad mood" or insinuate that they are somehow "unspiritual" and that a good quiet time and some prayer should get them "back on track." Bad moods will pass...depression won't.
- If they say they need some space, don't back off so much that you become absent. If they normally see/talk to you several times a week, and you stay away for weeks at a time out of fear or lack of understanding, this communicates the wrong thing.

The people who have provided this support to me over the years are priceless gems. Their love and kindness are a special kiss from God. I don't always know what I need, but I do know that the times when people give to me in these ways, it brings joy to my heart. You may be thinking you don't know where to begin or exactly what you should do. Pray, asking God for wisdom, and he will direct your heart and mind to give in the perfect way.

It may also be helpful to you to do some research on depression via the Internet or by checking out a book on the subject at your local library. The more you understand, the better you will be able to help.

All this may sound and feel like a lot to take in. My prayer is that you feel more hope and resolve in your journey to be well now than when you first began reading this chapter. Victory is possible, but not without God leading the way.

3

WRESTLING WITH SUFFERING

And we know that in all things God works for the good of those who love him and have been called according to his purpose.

Romans 8:28

The one thing we can be certain of at all times is that God is at work on our behalf. What has helped me over the years is looking for and recognizing the hand of God in each and every situation. When things are going great, it is very easy to see how our Father gives to us and loves us, and we very quickly give him thanks. We feel unworthy of all he bestows upon us.

It becomes more of a challenge to offer thanks when it feels like the bottom is falling out of our lives.

The apostle Paul tells us to "give thanks in all circumstances" in 1 Thessalonians 5:18. For me this means being aware of God at all times. For when I lose focus, I lose faith. The very real battle for our souls is happening twenty-four hours a day. Satan doesn't take vacation time when it comes to our destruction. But then again, neither do God and the legion of angels we have at our daily disposal. God has promised, "Never will I leave you; never will I forsake you" (Hebrews 13:5).

If we truly believe this, our lifestyles will be consistent

with our beliefs. The security that comes from identifying the hand of God reminds us that when things seem and feel impossible, we can be certain that they are not.

Perspective

Bryan and I have spent the majority of our lives as athletes. Bryan wrestled for thirteen years, eventually taking the NAIA title in 1985. He is now in the Wrestling Hall of Fame as well as the *Encyclopedia of American Wrestling* for his accomplishments. But long before God honored him in this way, he was just a small boy learning sportsmanship and socialization skills. He shared with me that he began wrestling when he was only ten years old. On his first day of practice, he said he was in pain and utterly exhausted.

He convinced himself that this was indeed the hardest sport known to man. Everything in him wanted to quit and find something less painful and more fun. The kind of training that is required of the human body to achieve top success in wrestling is overwhelming. The discipline required over the years became more and more difficult. He talked about having to run for miles straight up the side of a mountain until his legs ached so badly, he was sure they would become numb. His coach would have them run repeatedly up and down stairs with someone on their backs. They had to repeat wrestling moves over and over until they could do them in their sleep. To make weight before a match, he would have to run for miles in a plastic sweat suit while fasting at least two or three days prior to the event. Many times he wondered why he repeatedly punished his body in this way.

Then he would focus on the glory that came later. The trophies and titles that led to that ultimate championship helped him push through. Of course, this was all for personal glory and self-fulfillment. It wasn't until years later, when he became a Christian, that he was able to see how God used all of that training to produce discipline and self-control. God's hand was at work developing character and heart, the very things he would need to stay faithful in his lifelong spiritual journey.

One such time of spiritual testing came for Bryan back in 1987. His dad had to have surgery for a clogged artery to his heart. Shortly after the surgery, we received a phone call from the hospital saying everything was a success. We began to feel relieved and thankful. However, on his way to the recovery room, something began to go terribly wrong. His heart began to convulse and he died there on the table. He was the father of twelve children and not yet forty-eight years old.

Our feelings of relief and gratitude quickly vanished after receiving the second phone call. My husband began to ask God why. He was very close to his father and couldn't imagine his life without him. Before really having time to recover from this loss, a year later his sixteen-year-old brother was shot in his mother's driveway.

Some drug dealers were driving through the neighborhood and mistook his brothers for some other men. They pulled up to the house, and forced everyone facedown on the driveway. His brother in fear turned and ran for the front door, and they shot him on the porch. He ran a few steps farther into the house before collapsing in the hallway outside his mother's bedroom. She was awakened by this point and opened her bedroom door to discover her son lying dead at her feet.

How do you recover from severe trauma such as this? Amidst this level of pure horror, God says he will give us sufficient grace to get through it, but only if we're willing to persevere. Bryan shared with me that what pulled him through those tragedies was his dependence on God and his word, and the support and comfort of his relationships. Bryan was weak and turned to God, and God displayed his perfect power in this situation to make him stronger. He extended much grace to him through his relationships and family. Bryan refused to blame God, but chose instead to rely on him and all he knew to be true in his word to help him to move forward.

I don't believe God will always respond right away to our cries of help. There are times he will wait until we are in a position of complete surrender. He then responds with the exact amount of grace necessary to pull us through the trial. I think if we resist him *or* the lesson/challenge we are facing, it only takes longer for us to receive the necessary strength to achieve victory and growth. I believe that when we are weak, we are the most dependent on God and therefore in a position to receive real strength. That's why Paul was able to rejoice in those situations. In those moments we are most like Jesus.

We spend our whole life as Christians trying to be like Jesus, and then when God gives us opportunities to do so through hard times, we push them away and resist God. It's because we think we are most like Jesus in the "glory moments": Bible study, baptisms, helping others, teaching.... Those things are just an imitation of Jesus! We don't actually take on his characteristics or heart until we suffer. We can't get bitter and resent God when he opens a window of pain for us. He's allowing us the privilege of being as close to him as possible. If our focus is only on pain, we'll miss this.

Once we change our perspective and begin to view hardship as God does, we will be able to say with Paul that we too delight in weakness and hardship because we know what God will produce with them. It allows us to have hope during the crisis, and we know that "hope does not disappoint us" (Romans 5:5).

Loss

Pay attention to the details of each day, not over-looking anything. What appears to us as tedious or unimportant, may be something God is using to prepare us for what lies ahead. Over the years a countless number of women have shared their lives with me.

Some of their stories leave me weeping, wondering how any one person can survive so much. I see now that God has allowed each of us to have our experiences, just as they were, for a reason. There is a reason for your childhood being exactly as it was. There is a plan in God allowing certain people to have touched your life...whether for good or bad. We know from Acts 17 that God plans down to the finest detail our life circumstances. Our triumphs and successes as well as our tragedies and heartaches are all held tightly in the palm of God's hand. We must be able to say with David,

> You are my God.
>   My times are in your hands. (Psalm 31:14–15)

God has been watching over and orchestrating every event in your life thus far. Until we become convinced and secure in this knowledge, even the smallest of tests will overwhelm us, and the temptation of quitting will be that much stronger. Satan begins his celebration.

One of my closest friends, Pam Durkota, often comes to mind when I am tempted to be laid back and not allow Jesus to be Lord of all my circumstances. Pam and I first met over twenty years ago in Chicago and became casual acquaintances. Neither of us had begun our families yet. Now we both live in Atlanta and have children preparing for college. We reconnected a few years ago.

I recall bumping into her one particular Sunday after church, and I realized she was looking very sad. When I asked what was wrong, she told me she and her family had just returned from a trip to Illinois where she attended a funeral for five! Her husband's sister-in-law, her two children and his sister's two children were all killed when they were struck by a train in a railroad crossing. The sister-in-law's husband was the only survivor. They live in a very rural area, and these tracks had no gates or lights at the crossing to warn cars of an oncoming train. The area approaching the crossing was covered with brush on both sides so they were unable to see the train coming.

She spoke to me of the horror of having to visually take in five caskets at one funeral, with four of them belonging to small children. Five hearses were taken to the burial plots, and there were at least five hours of visitation the night before. Hundreds of people filled the high school gymnasium in this small town to mourn the loss of these family members. During the procession through town, people on the sides of the road stopped whatever they were doing, took off their hats, and held their hands over their hearts. People came out of store fronts and businesses to pay their respects as the procession went by.

It was all more than any one mind could process at the time. The enormity of what happened was too much to take in. The whole town grieved. But for Pam and John, the magnitude of it was much worse since these were their relatives.

John told me that it made him realize we are not immune to tragedy just because we are Christians. Tragedy is very real and can strike any one of us in an instant. It made him wrestle with his own mortality. However, he refused to allow Satan to destroy his belief in God in the process.

Although Pam has had to work through the emotional trauma that came as a result of such an ordeal, she has not become a defeated woman. On the contrary, she has become a very faithful, focused soldier of the cross. It is rare for me to ever have a conversation with her about anything where she doesn't mention God and what she has been studying about him lately. She consistently finds the good in circumstances and people, and she fights to keep the negative from entangling her mind or spirit. She's always first to offer a hug or word of encouragement to anyone else who may be suffering. She is always ready to share scriptures that might be helpful in any given situation. She seems very aware of the presence of God in her day-to-day life and is constantly thirsting to be closer to her Father in heaven.

I use her life often as a reference point because she is such a spiritual woman. She not only dealt with her own grief in this situation; she helped her three boys get through it as well. The people who know her and her family are quick to notice how compassionate and loving her children are. They are very others-centered. They haven't let this tragedy define them. I believe this speaks volumes about the kind of parenting and the depth of love in their home.

Pam is a woman of great conviction and tremendous faith. She has never questioned or blamed God for what happened on that tragic day, though if she had, God would have understood and would have helped her work it through. She still believes strongly in the cross and its power to transform us. The Word is her standard and God her closest companion. This is not something she told me; it is simply how she lives.

Many times I am far away from faith like hers. I am usually more focused on surviving life rather than living for God. In Philippians, Paul shares that he actually wants to know the fellowship of sharing in Jesus' suffering. To me, this sounds good in theory, and I know I should be there. It is what's right. However, trying to get my heart to follow my head can be extremely difficult. I too often fight God for control of my life.

> I want to know Christ and the power of his resurrection and the fellowship of sharing in his sufferings, becoming like him in his death, and so, somehow, to attain to the resurrection from the dead. (Philippians 3:10–11)

I don't want to know Christ above all else when life is painful. What I usually want more is relief from the storms of my life. I try to get as far away from suffering as I can. I silently hope God can teach me the same lessons some other way. Times when trials seem insurmountable are also the times when our reliance on God is most necessary. However, it is the least natural thing to do. James tells us,

> Consider it pure joy, my brothers, whenever you
> face trials of many kinds, because you know that
> the testing of your faith develops perseverance.
> Perseverance must finish its work so that you may
> be mature and complete, not lacking anything.
> (James 1:2–4)

I rarely consider trials a joy. To speak of trials being a joy can seem to be a contradiction in and of itself. I rarely find enough focus to look forward to what the trial is going to produce later. I'm too busy trying to understand why I am in the situation in the first place. I am trying to understand the reasoning behind it and figure out a point of rescue. I cannot partially persevere. I have to have total perseverance in order for God to make me both mature and complete. That means coming all the way through to the other end of the struggle.

Trying to bargain our way through a difficulty is pointless. We know we will never figure out God or his thinking. God says in Isaiah 55:9,

> "As the heavens are higher than the earth,
>   so are my ways higher than your ways
>   and my thoughts than your thoughts."

We don't get to see what God is thinking about us or our circumstances, not at the beginning, middle or the end. We are allowed to know as much as he decides we should know, and the rest is left up to trust…faith. If we have faith even the size of a mustard seed, we can move mountains, and God wants to work on our behalf. When we acknowledge our spiritual limitations and move out of our own way, faith can then do its work.

I am learning all over again that God gives without finding fault. When I'm weak or in sin, I've usually convinced myself that my prayers hold no power and that God doesn't want to hear from me, whereas the Bible teaches just the opposite in James 1:5–8:

> If any of you lacks wisdom, he should ask God, who gives generously to all without finding fault, and it will be given to him. But when he asks, he must believe and not doubt, because he who doubts is like a wave of the sea, blown and tossed by the wind. That man should not think he will receive anything from the Lord; he is a double-minded man, unstable in all he does.

Doubt destroys the blessing, not our sin. Our Father never wants us to question his ability. If he says something, it simply is! If we can allow the cross to be our center, the foundation during crisis, the Scriptures will come to life for us, and we will then see God's power in action.

Physical Illness

> As Jesus was on his way, the crowds almost crushed him. And a woman was there who had been subject to bleeding for twelve years, but no one could heal her. She came up behind him and touched the edge of his cloak, and immediately her bleeding stopped.

"Who touched me?" Jesus asked.

When they all denied it, Peter said, "Master, the people are crowding and pressing against you."

But Jesus said, "Someone touched me; I know that power has gone out from me."

Then the woman, seeing that she could not go unnoticed, came trembling and fell at his feet. In the presence of all the people, she told why she had touched him and how she had been instantly healed. Then he said to her, "Daughter, your faith has healed you. Go in peace." (Luke 8:42b–48)

Physical illness can be very challenging. From the time most of us were children, we have found illness, and even the thought of it, to be unsettling. All of us at one time or another have battled our share of colds and flu or even chicken pox or measles. If the illness hung on long enough, we remember in detail and can spin a fascinating recollection for anyone willing to listen. When I talk about the challenge of physical illness, I am referring to illnesses that are chronic and severe. This woman in Luke 8 had suffered for twelve long years. She had probably resigned herself to the fact that she'd always be ill, and just when she had all but given up hope, she met Jesus and he did for her what no else had been able to. He healed her.

I've had my share of challenges with sickness, but I am a little taken aback when I come in contact with people who have difficulties much worse than my own and yet manage to not only face them with courage and dignity, but to be steadfast in their commitment to God…and remain consistently joyful.

My friend Jacque Keen has this kind of joy. She has battled lupus for over thirty years now. Both her father and grandmother died from it, and she assumed she would die at a young age as well. She believed she would live for about four years after her initial diagnosis. She feared she would never marry or have a family. Deciding she would just honor God with whatever time she had left, she focused on her relationship with him and gave her life away to others to help them become Christians.

God had other plans for Jacque's life. She lived well past the four years, and God gave her the man of her dreams as well, her husband, Bob. Jacque soon found out that the second half of that dream (having children) was not going to be so easy. Because of the lupus, she miscarried twice. She later found out that one of the conditions of lupus was a blood clotting factor that was preventing her body from carrying a child full-term. Clots were forming in the umbilical cord.

God again kissed her, despite these setbacks, and she and Bob adopted their first child, Alicia. She now had her dream of a marriage and family. God also decided to grant them a miracle when she again became pregnant without complications and gave birth to their son, Brandon. Life was full and happy now.

Jacque experienced stability in her health for a number of years until 2003. That was when she was diagnosed with multiple sclerosis. As a result, she now has to deal with her legs and feet going numb due to brain lesions, and she has become partially blind as a result of one of the medications prescribed to supposedly help heal the lupus.

If you meet Jacque, you would never guess any of the above. She is one of the most joyful people I know. At times while sitting in church, I will look over at her and see her face beaming and her eyes alive with the Spirit's fire, and I am deeply humbled. She walks through the fellowship consistently giving to those around her. I don't believe I've ever seen her face downcast or her head hung low. I pray to be like her. I need so desperately to imitate her heart. Here is a woman for whom Nehemiah 8:10 holds true: "Do not grieve, for the joy of the Lord is your strength."

I sat down one day and asked Jacque how she does it. She shared with me that she wants to make a difference while she can. She has learned to rely on God more and not to look for security in her circumstances. Her relationship with God is her glue. He is the One she relies on. She believes God is faithful to her in every area. She doesn't focus on the negative or the illness and pain. Amazing! Proverbs 31:30 says, "A woman who fears the Lord is to be praised."

Jacque inspires me. I think of her often as an example of the type of woman I need to become. I praise God for her example and the examples of many like her who help me to stay in the fight and desire to be purehearted.

I believe that just as God's hand works at the peak of a crisis, he continues to be at work in ways we cannot see or understand. There have been times in my life when I didn't realize how God protected me until long after the difficulty has passed. For example, in Bryan's search for a job, he has been turned down several times for positions that appear to be the perfect fit, only to find out later that the company went under.

If we could understand the mind of God, he would not be God. One passage of Scripture that has encouraged me over the years is Psalm 139. I think of what our hands are used for: to comfort, to strengthen, to reassure and to express love. With this in mind, I read through this passage and circled the word "hand" every time it was used, referring to God's hand. I also noted the things it mentions his hands do for me: "guide me," "hold me," and "knit me." There is such detail and focus on me as an individual from the Lord's perspective that I walk away feeling completely loved and safe. I am better able to grasp how God's hand takes hold of my life. I can then be at peace during the most severe crisis.

Pain

One thing I have learned in wrestling with life is that God is trying to take me from where I am today, all the way to him. I believe the same to be true for you. Early on in my faith I was just as Paul describes in 1 Corinthians 13:11–12:

I talked like a child, I thought like a child, I reasoned like a child. When I became a man, I put childish ways behind me. Now we see but a poor reflection as in a mirror; then we shall see face to face. Now I know in part; then I shall know fully, even as I am fully known.

These spiritually immature levels of our hearts are for a limited time only. If we ever want to get to the point where we too will see God face to face, we have to expect suffering and allow God to train us to handle it. We will need to grow up in our faith and learn to see our lives as God sees them. I am learning that God's focus is not always on the crisis at hand, which is where mine tends to be. I can get so lost in the "storm," that I am no longer aware of the presence of God. The pressure of what is happening in my life can suffocate me because I allow my perception of it to become greater than my realization of what God can do. I believe he is working to knit my soul closer to his, to develop character and to teach me to rely heavily on him, to prepare me for my forever home with him. He doesn't get lost in the distraction of my personal pain.

When I was very young in my faith, God spent much time purifying my heart and peeling away the layers of the world that held me fast for so many years. The things I found difficult then are no longer a challenge for me. This is as it should be because God is allowing me to grow from one degree of glory to the next.

Early on, I had to focus on a daily basis not to give in to those sins that had enslaved me in the world:

lying, drunkenness, filthy language, impurity, and the like. Bad attitudes ran rampant in my heart because I lacked trust in any other living being. I was certain I would be betrayed and used. I looked for any little wrongdoing on the part of friends, and the minute I was hurt, I would hold their sin against them until I felt they deserved my forgiveness. How unlike Jesus I was.

As the years have gone by, those things are not much of a challenge for me, and Satan knows this. So he has to come up with things far more difficult for me to overcome. God also allows him this leverage because he knows I need to move past the elementary stages if I am ever to make it to heaven.

For some of us, heaven is a long way off yet. For others of us, it is imminent. We don't get to know which is true for whom. What we can be certain of is, the longer we're here on earth, the more difficult our lives will become. That's not to say we are to be miserable all of our days. There have been moments, days, weeks and sometimes months, that I wouldn't trade for anything in the world. It is true however, that the more you overcome, the more you have to overcome. If we quit anywhere along the way in our journey, it will all have been for naught. So we are asked to "leave the elementary teachings about Christ and go on to maturity" in the book of Hebrews.

I think that once we get past being shocked when things become increasingly difficult, and learn to expect this level of change, we will be more at peace during the challenge itself. We must get away from blaming God and stewing in anger every time we face something that we don't understand or is the least bit uncomfortable. Bitterness is a solid wall that keeps us from getting to God when we need him most, and also keeps him from being able to reach us. The responsibility is ours to remove it or prevent it from being built to begin with.

Set your spirit free of this burden of bitterness. For women, it is so easy to let our emotions lead us through life. They are so familiar and secure to us...even the disturbing ones. We think we trust and know ourselves better than anyone else. Our tendency, therefore, is to shoot from the hip, which is usually not in anyone's best interest. In Jeremiah 17:9, we learn that our hearts are "deceitful above all things and beyond cure." In a nutshell, God is saying, Don't trust your feelings.

Once Satan knows this is our tendency, he uses it against us during crisis. We only see our feelings and have taught ourselves to be secure giving into them. Satan and his legion of demons then proceed to distort things so that we begin to feel punished by God, and we begin looking for the wrongdoing on our part. We feel a need to find the loophole in his plan so that we can set it straight and in so doing, remove the horrible situation in which we find ourselves. We go off on an emotional goose chase.

In the end, we lose because we chose not to look for God and trust him in the midst of our troubles. Satan however, sits back and roars with laughter at our gullibility, while plotting his next scheme for us.

What we fail to recognize is that this is all so unnecessary. God simply asks this of us: "Be still, and know that I am God" (Psalm 46:10).

And he tells us through Exodus 14:14 as he told the Israelites: "The Lord will fight for you; you need only to be still."

If you are anything like me, you have just been asked the seemingly impossible. I don't know the meaning of the word "still." And I don't naturally know how to *be* it. My nature is one that is very anxious. As a child, I always had ten things going at once. Unfortunately, as an adult, I live the same way. I may get a call in the middle of the day, at which time I am not only then talking on the phone, but doing laundry, starting supper, and helping the children with their homework, all simultaneously of course. This does not seem the least bit abnormal to me. In fact, I feel certain that were the doorbell to ring at that very moment, I would invite inside whoever is there for a cup of coffee.

I have this need to feel productive every minute of every day. My pride kicks in, and somewhere in the background, I can hear Helen Reddy singing "I am woman, hear me roar."

To be in control is an amazing feeling to humans; it gives us a sense of power. Although control is good to have in some situations, in most issues we face as Christians, God asks just the opposite. He wants us to surrender that very thing so that he can work. So not only does it seem impossible to just be still physically, it truly takes an act of God on my behalf to get my spirit to do the same thing. There's that underlying thing called "fear" that kicks in when I hear such words as "surrender" or "yield." Handing over my life to another person is simply terrifying for me. However, each time I've done so with God, the end result always brings victory and peace. God is not man, and it will do us all good to capture this thought in our hearts. Most things we fear come from some life experience that we've allowed to train us to think in this manner.

We hold on to control to protect ourselves, and then we can't understand why we're not growing as quickly as we should. We follow our lists of things that guarantee a great relationship with God. We read and pray. We come to church and study the Bible with people, while denying ourselves daily and saying no to sin. So what seems to be the problem? We are not allowing God to be God. It is going to take 100% surrender of our spirits on a daily basis to see the kind of results we long for.

❄

Since God has allowed both physical and spiritual pain to become so frequent a part of my life over the last few years, I am learning to see it differently. Someone recently shared something with me that has been a tremendous help. I was telling them about some of the things our family has been going through and how I was so ready for a "break," for something "good" to come our way. This brother kindly said to me, "Dana, your life may never get easier. You may be one of those families chosen for difficulty. God may be using the trials of your family to bring glory to him. What if you never get that 'break'? Are you still going to love him?"

That was very sobering. I hadn't thought outside of the punitive realm so to speak. I had begun to question if I was under God's discipline more than his care. I had to decide then and there that no matter what he chooses for my life, I am resolved to love him for a lifetime.

4

WRESTLING WITH FAITH

So Shadrach, Meshach and Abednego came
out of the fire, and the satraps, prefects, gover-
nors and royal advisers crowded around them.
They saw that the fire had not harmed their bod-
ies, nor was a hair of their heads singed; their
robes were not scorched, and there was no
smell of fire on them.

Daniel 3:26b–27

The book of Daniel tells an amazing story of faith.
King Nebuchadnezzar's three administrators have been
given a challenge to bow down and worship the idol set
up in the king's name. The entire land had done so, and
they were expected to follow suit, especially since they
were leaders among the people. A great deal was at
stake for them. Not only were they to lose their positions should they refuse, they were to lose their lives. I
often wonder how many of us would have made the
choice they did. Would our faith really survive such an
intense testing? These men were very bold in their
response to the king's request for them to deny God.
That is exactly what they would have been doing had
they complied on any level. Their confidence in God
was secure, and when the king ordered them to bow
down or lose their lives, their response was:

"O Nebuchadnezzar, we do not need to defend ourselves before you in this matter. If we are thrown into the blazing furnace, the God we serve is able to save us from it, and he will rescue us from your hand, O king. But even if he does not, we want you to know, O king, that we will not serve your gods or worship the image of gold you have set up." (Daniel 3:16–18)

They were confident, that not only was God able, but he would indeed rescue them. They decided before they were thrown into the fire, that God would be in control of the outcome once there, even if he were to choose not to save them. There was never a moment's hesitation on their part. Regardless of the intensity of the flames or the personal pain suffered, they refused to sin or surrender to Satan even in their hearts.

If we aren't surrendered to God before a trial is at hand, we'll bow to Satan when threatened severely enough. If we find we're brave enough to actually face the fire on our own power, we will ultimately end up getting burned because we depended on ourselves to get us through it. And if we do come through the trial, the stench of fire will linger on us long afterwards. It will be obvious to all that we've been through a disaster because we're badly damaged. We'll lose heart and become easily discouraged. Sharing our faith with people will become a chore rather than a joy, and we will allow ourselves to feel that meeting with Christ's body, the church, is optional. The smell of smoke will be pervasive and will linger in our spiritual lives.

We have to decide, before the storms hit, to honor God before, during and after. We can't change our minds mid-stream due to the difficulty of the trial. Of course, this is easier said than done. But we need to remember that God's word doesn't change and his promises to us always remain the same. Therefore, we need to cling to them during the most critical times of testing as fervently as we would when things are going great. This is what assures us victory. Keep in mind however, that our refusal to surrender infuriates Satan, and he will make the fire he has intended to throw us into seven times hotter:

> Then Nebuchadnezzar was furious with Shadrach, Meshach and Abednego, and his attitude toward them changed. He ordered the furnace heated seven times hotter than usual and commanded some of the strongest soldiers in his army to tie up Shadrach, Meshach and Abednego and throw them into the blazing furnace. (Daniel 3:19–20)

The closer these men clung to God, the angrier the king became. The lesson for us is that the more we submit to God's plan for us during the trials he allows, the angrier Satan becomes with us. He will assign some of the strongest demons in his army to bind us, hoping to secure his victory and our defeat. We should be prepared for whatever challenge he initially planned to become increasingly more difficult and painful. Satan never will sit quietly by and watch our relationship with

God flourish and our faith grow. He is there to stop us any way he can, by any means necessary. The Bible tells us that the king's attitude toward these men changed. He went from entrusting them with responsibilities in his kingdom to executing the most excruciating death imaginable.

However, King Nebuchadnezzar was ultimately forced to bow before God as a result of their powerful example of faith. The decision made beforehand is what ultimately saved them. What brought them out of the fire not smelling like smoke is the fact that they had the same convictions coming out of the fire as they had going in! They made up their minds that God would bring about victory one way or another. The king took note after they had been rescued from the fire that "they trusted in him [God] and defied the king's command and were willing to give up their lives rather than serve or worship any god except their own God."

God humbled a nation of people through the example of these three men in their willingness to face the fire with confidence. In James 4:7–8, God promises us that if we resist Satan, he will flee. The way that we are to resist is by drawing near to God. We can't allow Satan's army to intimidate us during the difficult moments. These are the times our true character is exposed. Ephesians 6:16 tells us that our faith can extinguish *every* arrow Satan throws at us. It's easy to be led by emotion when life becomes difficult. We can't afford to let go of God's promises to us because if we lose sight, we lose the victory.

Facing the Fire

Several years ago, we experienced a horrible rainstorm that had some pretty severe lightning. There were warnings on TV and radio to take shelter because tornadoes had been spotted in the area. Our children were sleeping soundly in their rooms until an earth shattering noise shook the house and jolted them out of their beds. We heard yelling and what sounded like screams. We ran to the window to see who could possibly be outside during such treacherous weather. To the right of our house, in the center of the cul-de-sac, we saw our neighbor's house on fire with flames shooting to the treetops behind their house, illuminating the sky. It had been struck by lightning.

Our children quickly recognized that this was their friend's house and instantly began crying and worrying that he would not make it out alive. My husband and I quickly threw on our bathrobes, as did several other neighbors, and ran outside to help. The wife sat outside in the car with her two small children, ages two and four, in their pajamas watching as her husband dashed back and forth trying to salvage what he could before the entire house was completely engulfed. Nine months pregnant with her third child, she watched in disbelief as her home slowly became a pile of ashes while the firefighters were on their way. Even with the incredible torrential downpour, the rain was not coming fast enough to extinguish the flames that consumed the property. Once the firefighters were on the scene, it took at least another hour before all of the flames were extinguished.

After getting our family dry and settled for the night, we all turned in to try and sleep for the next few hours. The next morning smoke was still heavy in the air, and clouds of it hung over the house. For days afterward, the smell of smoke was very prevalent in our neighborhood. The family was not prepared for this kind of disaster. As far as they knew, they were planning for the new baby to be born in three weeks. They were decorating the nursery and enjoying baby showers and looking forward to this new addition to their lives. When they least expected it, the ultimate devastation happened. Everything lost in the fire had to be replaced and the house rebuilt.

Fire is no respecter of persons. It devours everything in its wake. When Satan throws you into the fire, he does not plan for you to come out. Since we never know when the fire in our lives will come, we have to be prepared.

Luckily for this family, insurance replaced everything they lost physically. But what about the emotional damage left behind? There is constant fear and insecurity that comes from having experienced the unknown. For us as disciples, we don't have to let fear control us. We have reason to trust that not only will God lead us out of the fire, he will be with us while we're in it.

We have to depend on God each and every minute of every day. This is always true for us as disciples, but God allows difficult times to remind us to go to him every morning for our "manna" to get through the day. As Christians, our convictions need to deepen and we need to become more determined to win the battle against Satan for our souls. In Hebrews 5:7, we learn that Jesus "offered up prayers and petitions with loud cries and tears to the one who could save him from death, and he was heard because of his reverent submission."

We have to be very careful where to direct our anger during hard times. Satan wants us to blame God and to become bitter and to feel abandoned. When indeed, we should be doing just the opposite. Be furious with him for having the audacity to try and snatch your soul and the souls of those you love. When life serves us blows we are not prepared for, it can catch us off guard leave us a little off balance. Fear can creep in and unsettle our spirits. Intense challenges can be very painful. We're human and we respond emotionally when we hurt. This is how God made us. But we can choose to respond in one of two ways:

1. We can get angry at God for allowing these things to happen or for not protecting us the way we think he should, or
2. We can get angry at Satan and remember who our real battle is against (Ephesians 6:10–18). Don't make it easy for Satan to lay you out. Put up a fight that lets him know you are in this for the long haul. In the book of Job, we see that Job refused to succumb to Satan's temptations

regardless of how bad things became for him. He was known by God as "a man who fears God and shuns evil." That is what made him such a tempting target for the devil. When your faith becomes challenging to the forces of evil in this world, you can be sure that you are a target for Satan.

I have a friend whose heart I often ask God to help me imitate. Her name is Lin Beaty. Her faith astounds me and her example is incredible. She has faced so much tragedy in her life, some of it back to back. She has had the bottom pulled out from under her life repeatedly, yet she remains forever connected to Jesus. Her eyes are always on the cross. She seems to be constantly seeking greater and better ways to serve God. She once told me that her biggest challenge is in wanting God to be enough for her. Her heart's desire is to serve him...period! The place of peace for her is to desire God, and him alone.

We sat on the phone for over an hour one day as she shared with me some of her hardships and how she has dealt with them. She began by telling me how completely devastated she was by the death of her husband, Barry. She allowed me a peek inside the beauty of her marriage. She spoke tenderly of the love affair she'd shared with her best friend for over twenty years before God called him home. A smile carried her voice as she shared about their lifestyle, their dreams, their home and family. She told me of Barry's strength, integrity and love for her and their children. I was able to see the kind of man he was and how God graced every aspect of his life. They worked side by side in the ministry and throughout their marriage. I was deeply moved as I listened because I'd never known Barry. But I could certainly understand the pain of losing my soul mate. Your one and only. Your only one.

Barry was diagnosed with a brain tumor in 1986. At the time, his prognosis was to live for one to five years. Lin came together with the church and all who loved them and begged God to extend Barry's life another fifteen years. God heard her desperate pleas, much like Hannah in the Bible. Barry was able to live another twelve years symptom-free before he became seriously ill. The last three years of his life were painful as his health continued to decline. He died exactly fifteen years later. God was very faithful to Lin in her prayer.

The heartache in all this was the giant hole it left in her life. Nothing felt familiar to Lin after Barry's death except her kids and the church. Having worked so long in the ministry together, she had become accustomed to his presence in all aspects of her life...at home during the day, at night, at church...everywhere. She did not have a job to escape to for eight hours a day to help give her a sense of routine and normalcy. She had to quickly learn to trust God as never before. She was now a single mother of three children—ages fourteen, eleven and six—who would need her desperately.

As if this were not enough, one of her brothers was diagnosed with the same type of tumor as Barry in

2002. He later died in 2004. That same year her dad also died of Parkinson's disease. Her mother has had breast cancer twice and skin cancer once. In the summer of 2007, her other brother died of cancer as well.

My heart breaks for Lin in so many places, so much of the time. Yet, when I look at her, she is certainly not a woman to be pitied. She is ever faithful to our God. She frequently asks people if she can do anything to serve them. When I think of her, I think of scriptures such as Philippians 4:4–7:

> Rejoice in the Lord always. I will say it again: Rejoice! Let your gentleness be evident to all. The Lord is near. Do not be anxious about anything, but in everything, by prayer and petition, with thanksgiving, present your requests to God. And the peace of God, which transcends all understanding, will guard your hearts and your minds in Christ Jesus.

She doesn't walk around looking frazzled. I remember saying to her, "Lin, how are you even standing at this point?"

She said simply, "God is all I have. He's all any of us have when it's all said and done. The church is home for me. Coming here gives me strength and comfort." She told me she learned this about suffering: "It does not matter what you're going through at the time. It has more to do with where you are spiritually when you are going through it." What an amazing insight! I realized as she said this how true it is. When I'm close to God and living in submission to the cross, trials are a lot easier to face. When I drift and begin to depend on myself for strength, the load I'm carrying seems ten times heavier.

Lin said her most fervent desire is to be known simply as a woman who walked with God. If at the end of her life, this is how she is remembered, she feels she will have honored God with her time here on earth. Those of us who are privileged to be her friends know she is certainly who she desires to be—a woman who walks with God.

I don't know why hearing the stories of other women's heartache shocks me so. It seems they have been given more than their share of difficulty. It certainly doesn't seem fair...that is, until I take time to look into God's word and remember that they are not the first. They will not be the last. Paul's story was much like that of my sisters in Christ. Listen as he shares with the church in Corinth.

> Are they servants of Christ? (I am out of my mind to talk like this.) I am more. I have worked much harder, been in prison more frequently, been flogged more severely, and been exposed to death again and again. Five times I received from the Jews the forty lashes minus one. Three times I was beaten with rods, once I was stoned, three times I was shipwrecked, I spent a night and day in the open sea, I have been constantly on the move. I have been in danger from

rivers, in danger from bandits, in danger from my own countrymen, in danger from Gentiles; in danger in the city, in danger in the country, in danger at sea; and in danger from false brothers. I have labored and toiled and have often gone without sleep; I have known hunger and thirst and have often gone without food; I have been cold and naked. Besides everything else, I face daily the pressure of my concern for all the churches. (2 Corinthians 11:23–29)

Later in chapter 12, verse 10, Paul says: "For when I am weak, then I am strong." I believe the reason God allows us to go through so much is not so that we can feel isolated and attacked. It is not to tempt us to quit. It is so that God can strengthen us. When we are weak, we are more vulnerable. That's when we're most likely to hear the Spirit speaking in that gentle whisper to our souls. We are more prone to being taught and to obeying those things in Scripture that seem a little outside our realm of comfort. We let down our guard (that is, our pride), and now God can work.

It's very hard to remember that brothers and sisters throughout the world are also suffering when we are in the midst of our own trials. That's why it is so encouraging to share our lives with each other. Sharing in the lives of the women I have written about in this chapter makes it more possible for me to be faithful in my own life. It helps me put things into perspective. Whatever it is God may be allowing you to experience in your life at this time, take heart in knowing you are not alone.

Maybe sharing your experience with others will give them the courage they need to face their own battles. Let God work and don't give way to fear.

Lin reminded me that we all live on borrowed time, and we need to make the most of it. She said the key is to be sure I'm holding on to the right hand. Even if you think you can't handle any more, God can and he will, as long as it is his hand that we're holding.

We learn from the story in Daniel that there are varying degrees of heat once we are thrown into the fire. Maybe for some of you the fire has not yet been made very hot, and for you the story of Daniel seems fairly extreme. For others of us, we relate all too well with the furnace being turned seven times hotter than its original temperature. Regardless of your perspective, be assured, you will face the fire, and each time you do, the temperature gets a little hotter.

We must trust that even when the fire is burning with the highest intensity, God is still in control and eager and ready to rescue us from the blaze. The challenge for us is always to be prepared before the smoke ever rises to have convictions that will never change regardless of what Satan has in store for us.

Seeking Patience

God does not give us a fast food menu where we can just order what we want him to do. In our world of fast-paced technology, we've become accustomed to having what we want right now. Standing beside a microwave waiting for water to heat for a couple of minutes feels like an eternity to us. "What is wrong with this machine?" we may ask ourselves. It must be getting old because it used to get things hot much quicker.

With e-mail, we can communicate with people around the world within seconds. The same holds true for fax machines, telephones and cell phones. We don't even have to pull over in the car to get out and use a pay phone should our plans change during the day. We can continue driving to our destination while taking care of our next appointment, all without missing a beat.

Now don't get me wrong, I enjoy the twenty-first century just as much as the next person. I just think there is something to be said about what we learn from our heroes in the Bible and their lifestyles. Everything they did took time. They couldn't just whip up a meal in twenty minutes. They began with hunting! Imagine having to start there every time you got hungry. They were accustomed to having to wait for life to unfold. As a result, I think they enjoyed what they had with God all the more. It wasn't as much of a stretch for them to wait on God. Sitting still was a normal part of your day if you were a shepherd or maybe a fisherman. My concern is that, for many of us, we will miss out on the peace God is offering because we've become too dependent on things and people to gain the results we want.

Let's get back to having a heart that is trained by

patience rather than technology. The writer of Hebrews tells us to remember our leaders, those who have gone before us, and "consider the outcome of their way of life and imitate their faith" (v7). Keep in mind that the Bible is not an entertaining storybook, but our family legacy as disciples. Who we are and who we will become is laid out for us on every page.

Jeremiah taught us that our lives are not our own, and it is not for us to direct our steps (Jeremiah 10:23). I find it helpful to study the lives of great men and women in the Old Testament. I suggest that you look at Moses, Joshua, Daniel, Job, Esther, Jeremiah, Ruth and David. Walk through their journeys with them, and pay attention to all the times God called them to wait for his guidance, and then see the results that came with doing so.

Their stories amaze and inspire us. But they were people just like you and me, and if God can change the world with them, I believe he can do the same with us. We just have to step aside and allow his hand to guide us. And maybe one day in the generations to come, our children's children will learn from how we sat still and waited on God, and how his hand delivered us again and again.

Finding Blessings

I've spent the majority of this chapter sharing about the challenging side of finding God's hand in our lives. I don't however want to neglect to mention the best part of this topic…the blessings. I happen to be of the mindset that if you are a disciple of Jesus, a child of God for whom heaven awaits, that God makes a special effort to encourage you on a daily basis.

If you are a parent, think of how often your kids are on your mind and how often you are either planning something special for them or actually doing something involving them. The same holds true for God where we are concerned. Now you may be thinking that with so much difficulty taking place in your life right now, you find it hard to believe that God is thinking about you all the time. I've been there. Satan does not want us to believe this so that we will miss the blessings God sends our way.

Sometimes God just flat out encourages us on a grand scale with maybe a family member becoming a Christian or with us buying a new home, or maybe we get an incredible job opportunity that we've been praying about. On those occasions we have to be sure to acknowledge God with praise and thanksgiving.

Sometimes God just allows our day to go well from beginning to end. Maybe he is keeping our family all healthy and strong. Or he is adding to our lives new friends that bring joy, vision and confidence. At times, it can be our children and the fact that they are thriving and achieving positive growth in all areas of their lives. Or perhaps it could be something as little as saving that parking space right in front of the grocery store just for you when you're running short on time. Before you laugh at that one...I actually say a prayer thanking God every time this happens to me.

The same holds true for me when I do mundane things such as laundry. My brothers and sisters in other countries don't have piles of laundry because they only own a few outfits. I have more than enough. I try and train myself to say prayers of thanks throughout the day for what may appear to be the smallest of things. I find it keeps my heart at that "squishy" stage with God. I feel closer to him, more aware of him, and I find it easier to talk to him when things become difficult. I love it when people encourage me, and since I'm created in God's image, I figure he must feel that way as well.

If we can find a way to hold on to those things we know to be true in our lives regardless of how we feel, it will be much easier to connect with the blessings. It is always true that God loves me, even if my emotions try to tell me otherwise. It is always true that he is working for my good as Romans 8 teaches. These two things alone allow me the freedom to search my experience to find those special things that come just from my Father.

5

WRESTLING TO PERSEVERE

"Fear not, for I have redeemed you;
  I have summoned you by name; you are
    mine.
When you pass through the waters,
  I will be with you;
And when you pass through the rivers,
  they will not sweep over you.
When you walk through the fire,
  you will not be burned;
  the flames will not set you ablaze."

Isaiah 43:1b–2

What a tremendous scripture this is to help us know how well God cares for us. I must have read this verse dozens of times during some of the lowest periods in my life. I desperately needed the assurance of not only knowing God is there during those black hours, but that he cares about what is happening to me. I am God's and he is with me. That's all the assurance I need.

Sometimes when the challenges we face seem to overwhelm us, we can't always see clearly enough to even imagine moving beyond our present situation.

God is always there with and for us! Satan likes to deceive us into believing we're all alone during the difficult moments because that's what our feelings tell us.

Our feelings are not always a reliable barometer of God's presence during trials.

God takes care of us in ways that we are very often not even aware of. Looking back over our most recent set of challenges, I am aware of God paving the way some twenty years ago for us. How is that possible you may ask? Well, as a young teen, God allowed me to get to know Larry and Mary Lou Craig. I spent seven years in their lives, in and out of their home, babysitting, house sitting, getting dating advice, and adapting to campus life under their tutelage. They are friends I hold close to my heart. So many of my favorite memories include them.

Now fast forward to where my husband and I are in Atlanta as we face some of the toughest times in our Christian faith to date. We have relied on several friends for strength, comfort and encouragement. Two of those friends were the Craigs. They were living in New York at the time and could not physically be there for us, but Mary Lou let us know that she had a sister who lived in Atlanta—Jane Whitworth. She thought Jane and her husband, Clyde, would be able to help guide us through our trials at the time.

Bryan and I were able to meet with them and share what we were going through, and indeed, they did help. In fact, Jane gave us some life-saving scriptures that we both had quiet times on for the next couple of months. These verses provided countless hours of hope and peace. I've listed them for you in hopes that they may do the same for you.

Genesis 50:20	Psalm 91:4
2 Chronicles 20:17	Psalm 94:18–19
Job 42:2, 5	Psalm 102:2
Psalm 13	Psalm 119:75–76
Psalm 18:30–32	Isaiah 43:1–7
Psalm 22:19	Isaiah 46:4
Psalm 27:13–14	Isaiah 49:14–15
Psalm 31:22	Isaiah 54:10
Psalm 34:4–7	Isaiah 63:9
Psalm 37:7a	Lamentations 3
Psalm 46:10	John 16:33
Psalm 50:15	Romans 8:28–39
Psalm 68:19	2 Thessalonians 3:16
Psalm 71	Hebrews 1:14

I was so encouraged to see that God went to such great lengths to comfort us. And that he began preparing the way for our victory many years before.

Even though it may take more effort to go after God when life is rough, we have to make our time with him a priority. Don't let Satan deceive you into setting aside the Bible when you are hurting. We may ask, "God, where are you?" He hasn't moved. He's in his word and in disciples around you, waiting to love and help you through whatever it is you are facing.

I can recall a particular period when things had become very grim for me and having regular quiet times was a struggle. I was driving down the road in my car, and I remember praying simply this: "God, come and get me. I am having such a hard time getting to you. Please help me." That was the extent of my prayers for that entire day. But it was a prayer of faith, coming out of desperation, and God heard my cry, as he promises he always will:

> The righteous cry out, and the LORD hears them;
>   he delivers them from all their troubles.
> The LORD is close to the brokenhearted,
>   and saves those who are crushed in spirit.
> (Psalm 34:17–18)

Not long after that, God put a couple in our life who not only were able to help us, but also understood what we were going through—James and J.J. Currie.

An example of J.J.'s heart that allowed me to see Jesus was when I had to fly home to be with my mother in the summer of 2000. She was in the critical care unit with a team of five specialists working on her. I had an early flight at 8:00 AM, and J.J. drove out to the airport during rush hour (45 minutes out of the way) when she had to be at work at 9:00. She arrived ten minutes before my flight took off, and I had already boarded the plane. In tears, she explained my situation to one of the flight attendants, asking if she would find me and give me a gift. Amazingly, the attendant was willing to deliver her gift to me (despite the airport policy of not taking anything on the plane that someone you didn't know had given you).

J.J. had put together a week's worth of quiet times for me...knowing my mind was too scattered to focus.

She also put a candle in the bag along with a note reminding me to be the "aroma of Christ" to those around me. That single gesture of love was the very thing I needed to get me through that week.

God did answer that single prayer along the road that day. He spoke to me through his word. He used other people's love for him and their love for me to help. He used my husband and children. And the best part was, he answered quickly.

We are not meant to carry the weight of our problems alone. Rely on your friends. Allow them to be close to you during the difficult moments. It will make all the difference.

Grasping for Hope

> Therefore we do not lose heart. Though outwardly we are wasting away, yet inwardly we are being renewed day by day. For our light and momentary troubles are achieving for us an eternal glory that far outweighs them all. So we fix our eyes not on what is seen, but on what is unseen. For what is seen is temporary, but what is unseen is eternal. (2 Corinthians 4:16–18)

Perseverance is the thread, so to speak, in Christianity that keeps everything connected. It's what gets us from one day to the next. It's what turns the days into weeks, the weeks into months, and the months into years.

Unfortunately, the only way to learn true perseverance

is to suffer. That's what Paul teaches us in Romans. I'm not quite sure what the dynamic is and how it works. I just know for me, when I am suffering I am always faced with two choices. I can either go through the suffering until God brings me to the other side, or I can quit, that is, just give up my faith. It's as simple as that. Lucky for us there is no gray area. I don't ever give myself a back door. There is no alternate escape route. I made up my mind long ago that being a Christian was a lifelong decision. That cinches the deal no matter what lies ahead.

That's not to say I've never felt like quitting. I certainly have been tempted when things have been incredibly difficult. But because that has already been ruled out as an option, the only choice I'm left with is making it through to the other side. It then becomes a matter of vulnerability and surrender on my part to both God and man.

In 2 Corinthians 12:7–10, Paul writes,

> To keep me from becoming conceited because of these surpassingly great revelations, there was given me a thorn in my flesh, a messenger of Satan, to torment me. Three times I pleaded with the Lord to take it away from me. But he said to me, "My grace is sufficient for you, for my power is made perfect in weakness." Therefore I will boast all the more gladly about my weaknesses, so that Christ's power may rest on me. That is why, for Christ's sake, I delight in weaknesses, in insults, in hardships, in persecutions, in difficulties. For when I am weak, then I am strong.

What an amazing mindset to have. If you're anything like me, your first reaction to this is something along the lines of, "Who in their right mind thinks like this?" Apparently Paul did, and it took him all the way to heaven. I do not like pain of any sort...ever. It's not something I relish or look forward to. So for me to delight in what I perceive to be misery does not compute in my brain on any level. But after studying this passage further, God allowed me to see why Paul came to view things in his life this way.

First of all, God allows suffering and difficulty to keep us humble and close to him. That's how he is able to lead and direct our lives. Paul said he had been able to experience some pretty amazing things in his life, and God wanted to keep him from becoming conceited. The same holds true for us. When things start to go incredibly well in our lives, our tendency is to think *we* are accomplishing these things ourselves. God did this to Paul to keep him focused and to give him some perspective about where things really were.

Paul begs God to take away what was tormenting him rather than ask for the courage to face it and get through it. Our response tends to be much the same. God's response however is that "his power is made perfect in weakness."

As a young athlete, I learned many lessons about perseverance. At first, I hated it. Pain has never been my friend...even if potential glory awaits me at the end. I mentioned earlier that I ran track for a number of years and swam competitively as well. Although I enjoyed the pleasures of these sports, the discipline it took to succeed in them was not always welcome. I can recall a time when I fractured my hipbone and had shin splints in both legs as well. I was determined not to let this stop me from competing because I had my heart set on the state track championships.

In order for my legs to be able to handle the constant, daily pounding on the track, I had to sit in a tank filled with ice up to my hips several times a week. (Yes, that is as completely unpleasant as it sounds.) I went through a myriad of changes to force myself to stay in the tank. At first, it's just horrible. You're frozen and in pain…not a good combination. But your limbs quickly go numb. If you can train yourself to push through until you hit this level, it doesn't seem as bad. (At least that's what I used to tell myself…work with me.)

Sometimes more than one of us would have to sit in there, and it helped to have a little company to commiserate with you. The time passed quicker, and we felt a sense of camaraderie in our "torture." I'm not sure how exactly this helped to heal my limbs, but it did. I ran with my ankles taped, my shins wrapped and my hip numb, all for worldly glory. The physical discipline I learned back then has since taught me many things about spiritual discipline. I think of the scripture in 1 Corinthians 9:25–27 which says:

> Everyone who competes in the games goes into strict training. They do it to get a crown that will not last; but we do it to get a crown that will last forever. Therefore I do not run like a man running

aimlessly; I do not fight like a man beating the air. No, I beat my body and make it my slave.

If I was willing to go through all of that for a crown that will not last, how much more should I be willing to endure to wear a spiritual crown?

I know a woman here in Atlanta named Sharon Waller; she is a great example of perseverance. She found out in August 1992 that she had lupus. At the time she had a fifteen-month-old baby named Nick. God allowed her to meet and study with Christians shortly after receiving this devastating news, and she too became a follower of Jesus soon afterwards at the age of thirty-eight.

At the time of her diagnosis Sharon was working as a supervisor in a word processing center earning close to $32,000 a year. Two years later, she found herself severely ill and unable to work at all. She lost her job, had zero income, and had a three-year-old son to raise. She came down with bronchitis and pneumonia. The lupus started affecting her lungs and heart, and it caused swelling of the tissue lining in her brain. She was very close to death. Certain she would die, she could not see how God would take care of her and her young son.

But God always has a plan. He handpicked the pulmonary specialist, the neurologist and the cardiologist who all worked to pull her through that crisis. Her heavenly Father also made sure there were Christians in her life to take care of her day-to-day needs and those of Nick.

The toll her circumstances took on her brought on severe clinical depression that required additional medication. In 1995 she developed the muscular/skeletal disease known as fibromyalgia. This illness brought on swelling in her muscles and joints, along with back pain and heart palpitations. Because of the nature of the disease, it triggers the symptoms of lupus, which in turn brings on the depression.

Over the years, her situation has not changed much. If anything, it has become more difficult. She is on a number of daily medications. There are days when she cannot walk, cook or even speak coherently. She often had people take Nick into their homes for "sleepovers" because she was unable to care for him.

Her situation sounds horrendous to most of us, and I'm sure it is certainly challenging. But anyone who knows her, knows that quitting is never an option for her. The word doesn't exist in her vocabulary. God has provided her with a monthly income to meet their needs. Although she receives substantially less than when she was able to work, she never complains about her income. She lives within her means and thanks God for each day he grants her. Many days she is unable to attend church or even be around people because of her immune system. People cannot visit her if they even have so much as a cold because that could be detrimental to her fragile health.

However, she calls to encourage people, and when

she can, she serves. Her son is in high school now. She accepts nothing as an excuse. She always finds a way around things because she has had to. Her heart and her life challenge me to fight hard to make it to the other side. I am grateful for a friend like her who is a constant reminder to not just suffer through things, but to push through with faith.

Looking for Joy

Consider it pure joy, my brothers whenever you face trials of many kinds. (James 1:2)

Sharon and I have been friends for several years now. I've often thought I could never make it through a situation even remotely like hers. During the course of writing this book, God proved just the opposite to be true by allowing me to be in a very similar circumstance. This time, however, the difficulty came in the duration of my hardship as opposed to the intensity of it.

In November of 2001, I came down with what I thought was a severe case of the flu. I spent four weeks in bed with fever, vomiting, sore throat, headaches and very crippling body pain. Two weeks into this episode, I went to the doctor and was told I had mononucleosis and would spend another two to three weeks in bed and should be back to myself fairly soon except for some lagging fatigue.

Well, two months later, I was no better. I was discouraged, frustrated and sick and tired of being sick and tired. This time I learned from my doctor that the episode of mono I had was so intense that it had escalated into Epstein-Barr syndrome and would hang on for another month or two; then I could expect to gradually feel better.

By the fifth month of continued illness, my doctor realized something very different was going on and had me referred to an infectious disease specialist as well as a rheumatologist. I tested positive for lupus in March 2002, although some of my symptoms were not completely consistent with that disease.

Eventually more tests had to be ordered, including an MRI on my brain because I had also begun having frequent dizzy spells that would momentarily blur my vision. The doctors needed to rule out multiple sclerosis or any possibility of a brain tumor. Fortunately, all of the tests came back negative.

A second antinuclear antibody test (ANA) for lupus was ordered to see if my cell count had changed. This time, the test came back negative. Of course, this was very good news. One doctor, however, was able to figure out that I do have fibromyalgia and this was not likely to go away anytime soon. Most people diagnosed with this illness must struggle with it for their lifetime.

In the beginning, I couldn't make it a full thirty days consecutively without running a fever. I couldn't make it an entire week without my body being racked with pain. My muscles would swell, my joints throb. I had constant headaches, earaches and the continued dizziness. I had to quit my job. There were days when I couldn't even sit up in the mornings to get out of bed.

I had to first lie on ice, take medication and allow that to work its way through my system for a good thirty minutes before I could get up. To this day, I need five different prescription medications just to make it through most days. I've come to terms with the fact that this is something I may have to deal with on a permanent basis. I try to find the good in what is happening so that I can be refreshed and have a greater sense of connection with God.

I believe the reason God has me at this point in my life, is so that I will realize my need for him and not depend on my own abilities. I realize as Paul did that God has delivered me again and again, and he is not going to abandon me now. It's become clear to me that as long as I'm depending on him, the burden never becomes too much to bear.

When I try to handle the weight or intensity of it all on my own, it becomes overwhelming and I feel stressed out. When viewed through God's perspective, the challenges he allows in my life are light, an easy burden when carried by him. For those of you who face physical limitations or also suffer with a chronic illness, take heart and take hold of this scripture. Meditate on it day and night as the Psalms teach us:

> But his delight is in the law of the LORD,
>   and on his law he meditates day and night.
> (Psalm 1:2)

It will bring you both peace and freedom. They give birth to joy.

Appreciating Relationships

Our relationship with God is the most precious blessing we have. It is the heart of our spiritual foundation. Everything else must be built around it. It is the one true thing worth fighting for at all times, no matter what we're going through. Without it, any other facet of spiritual structure we try to implement in our lives will crumble. He is to be our "first love," as Jesus said to the church at Ephesus:

> You have forsaken your first love. Remember the height from which you have fallen! Repent and do the things you did at first. If you do not repent, I will come and remove your lampstand from its place. (Revelation 2:4–5)

I have had to challenge myself to get back to my first love and to do the things I did at first when it comes to my times with God. I notice that as the years have gone by, my convictions in this area have begun to weaken. I don't push myself as hard to make sure I have a daily time with God that actually changes who I am. I let myself get away with just reading and praying some days instead of actually studying God's word. Even in the course of writing this book, I have allowed myself to be distracted by the many demands in my schedule and have sacrificed my time with God to "being busy." That wasn't an acceptable excuse when I started out and it certainly is not now.

My schedule and life may have become a lot more

demanding as the years have gone by, but the thing that should not change is my heart and my attitude about my time with God. As long as we have the mind-set that our daily times with God are "optional" or that five out of seven days aren't bad for a week, we will continue to stunt our own spiritual growth.

I am so challenged by my husband, who has always maintained this as his strength. He has been a Christian for twenty-four years and has never missed a quiet time! When you're finished gasping for air (yes, it's a little mind blowing to me too), decide along with me to allow yourself to be humbled enough to imitate his conviction. Bryan is the least legalistic person I know, and I say that because it can appear that his commitment can come simply from an obligation of some sort. I've often asked him how he has been able to maintain this. His response is "Honey, if Jesus need-ed regular time with God and he was perfect, how can I afford to do with any less?" Well, all righty then! Enough said...next!

Paul writes in 1 Corinthians 3:10–15:

> By the grace God has given me, I laid a founda-tion as an expert builder, and someone else is building on it. But each one should be careful how he builds. For no one can lay any founda-tion other than the one already laid, which is Jesus Christ. If any man builds on this foundation using gold, silver, costly stones, wood, hay or straw, his work will be shown for what it is, because the Day will bring it to light. It will be

> revealed with fire, and the fire will test the quality of each man's work. If what he has built survives, he will receive his reward. If it is burned up, he will suffer loss; he himself will be saved, but only as one escaping through the flames.

The older I get as a Christian, the more I realize the need for a solid foundation. Starting over with young children again as I approach my fifties is challenging to me. My memory is not what it used to be. I find myself trying to instill in my two youngest children those things most necessary to give them a good start in life. I don't remember *how* I taught the two oldest or *when*. However, I do know enough to realize the basics are essential for them.

The same holds true spiritually. I work harder at helping my friends solidly lay the groundwork of their faith. I hear myself sharing about the cross of Jesus more and more because I think this is the core of a good foundation. It's the center and heart of Christianity. I pray with people more than just telling them to pray. I share my quiet times with people as a means of encouragement, yes, but also to teach them how to do this for themselves.

We need each other. None of us can make it to heaven on our own. There are numerous passages in the Bible that teach us to "encourage one another,""pray for each other," "build one another up," "serve one another" and so on. We all need relationships that last us a lifetime and pull us through life's storms.

I am so grateful to so many of my friends who were there for me during the most difficult of times. I often give prayers of thanks to God for their faith and for their love for him. I praise God for allowing them to go through all they've been through, which has put them in a position to now help me. Paul teaches us in 2 Corinthians 1:4 that we should comfort those in trouble "with the comfort we ourselves have received from God." What a powerful and reassuring passage. How comforting it is to know that we can rely on each other's wisdom and life experience. I am so grateful for those Christians who have wells that run deep when it comes to love, comfort and strength. They seem to never run out of what those around them are in need of. Our God is an awesome God!

I am thankful for those who took the time to help my friends build strong foundations and who pulled them through vicious storms, eased their pain and comforted their hurts. Their healing provides opportunities for them to love me when my faith is tested. This is God's design for each of us. I have friends that have been a part of my life for over two decades and others whom I cherish that I've gotten to know in the last ten or fifteen years. The joy in this is that no matter where we live, no matter where our lives take us, we are always there for each other. We see each other through the best and worst of times, and we all need this kind of support. We can all have this kind of support. It is certainly not beyond our reach in the Lord's church.

In Romans 8:38–39, Paul describes the depth of

God's love for us. He says that nothing can separate us from our Father's love—not life, death, angels, demons, the present or the future. Since God's love lives in each of our hearts as his disciples, it makes sense that the same would hold true in our relationships with each other. Time and distance are not determining factors for us. We can and should be there for each other on the most deep and personal levels. It is rare to find even one friend in the world that will stand by your side throughout your lifetime. It is the hand of God that offers you several.

Take time to enjoy your friends. Let's become like our brother Paul who taught us in Philippians 2:3 to "consider others better than yourselves." If each of us is putting someone else's needs ahead of our own, we will all be emotionally full and spiritually happy. The Scriptures also teach us in 1 John 3:16 that just as Jesus "laid down his life for us, we ought to lay down our lives for our brothers." Let's give our best in imitating our Lord.

6

HEAVEN

We are confident, I say, and would prefer to be
away from the body and at home with the Lord.
2 Corinthians 5:8

Being at home with the Lord is something I long for
with everything in me. I daydream and fantasize about
heaven. I imagine what it will look like. I imagine what
it will feel like. I allow it to be very real to me. I try and
capture it with as much as my five senses will allow. I
think of all of my favorite things, and I know they'll be
there. I think of the most beautiful places here on
earth, their grandeur, splendor and majesty. Then I
stop and think that if God allows me to enjoy this while
on earth, what has he planned or prepared for me in
heaven?

> "I am going there to prepare a place for you.
> And if I go and prepare a place for you, I will
> come back and take you to be with me that you
> also may be where I am." (John 14:2–3)

I love water scenes—beautiful oceans, waterfalls,
lonely lighthouses sitting above a rocky crest, sandy
shores with waves crashing against the rocks. I love the
smell of salt air, the cerulean color of island waters,

with depths so crystal clear you can see clean through to the tropical sea life below.

I love mountains, green and lush, high and majestic. I enjoy watching the colors of the leaves turning in the fall as their beauty is transformed with the gentleness of a breeze. I love their appearance when they are snow capped. I love the imagery of crystal streams flowing through them in winter. The beauty they provide is overwhelming. I can almost taste the fresh flowing water as it rushes through and around a frozen mountaintop. If you stop and listen, the only sounds heard are the whispers of God.

I think of the beauty of our world—the Swiss Alps, Italy, France, Spain, Australia and Africa. These are some of my favorite countries with breathtaking beauty in their landscape. I stop to think of what it would be like to visit every place I love, places I visit only in books or magazines.

If I just had all the time I wanted to explore ancient ruins or historic castles, or maybe Egyptian pyramids. If I could travel from one continent to another for the purpose of pure pleasure, what would that be like? No time constraints…money being no obstacle. What an enormous treat. It might take months, maybe even years. That would be fabulous, and this is just to enjoy the pleasures of this earth.

I imagine God just gave us tidbits here. I believe heaven is more than we can even dream. I don't think we can fathom or conjure up the kind of beauty in store for us there. It's beyond our grandest fantasies.

And we will have endless amounts of time to explore and enjoy. And these are just the visual aspects.

Friends

We also get to fellowship with all those who have gone before us. Imagine having coffee with Jesus. I imagine this because I enjoy coffee more than just about all of the treats God created for us. Imagine going out for a prayer walk on a beautiful oceanside with Mary just to get to know her? Imagine having dinner with Daniel and asking him what it was like living on fruits and veggies during all that time? How about having a great time with Paul, no interruptions because time is not a factor? And you get to have him all to yourself because he isn't keeping an agenda.

Anticipate that first moment when you see your friends and relatives who made it there before you. What do you think you'll talk about? Maybe they can be a tour guide and show you around their most exciting spots.

I remember when our daughter Briana was eight years old; she had a dream that greatly encouraged her. It was so special to her that if you ask her about it to this day (she's nineteen now), she will recall it in vivid detail. She dreamed that she came home from school one day, and as she was coming up the driveway, Jesus was standing there waiting for her and gave her a hug. He knelt down to her level, so as to be able to stare her in the eyes and said simply, "Come with me."

He took her by the hand and they floated up to heaven. When she got there, she said she saw a room for each of our family members, and inside each one were all of our favorite things. She said in Mommy's room was lots and lots of coffee. In Daddy's room, there were all kinds of athletic equipment. In Travis's room, everything was football. In her room, there was a giant canopy bed with pink and white lace and ruffles, dolls and pillows. She then got to walk around heaven and meet people. She met Mary and Moses and said she got to sit down with them and eat macaroni and cheese (Mommy's kind and not the kind in the box). I later asked her who gave them the recipe...and she said they just knew. Since it was her favorite thing, or course it was there. She never questioned it.

She talked about several biblical figures she talked with and even mentioned what they wore. A couple had on T-shirts with cool pictures of Jesus on them. After a while, Jesus came and got her, saying it was time to go back now. She was sad because she wanted to stay. He brought her back to the driveway and before leaving, took her face in his hands and said, "You all are the best family; you know what to do." And then he was gone.

That dream came when our family was facing some very difficult times, and so it became a comfort to us all. The thing she was not aware of, but that I never forgot, was that exact scripture about Jesus going and preparing a place for us. And so he did, with all of our favorite things. God went to great lengths to encourage our daughter by helping his word come alive for her. For approximately six months before the dream, she had been experiencing some pretty severe nightmares and had not been sleeping through the night. After that dream, they never returned.

At Home with Daddy

In 2 Corinthians 5:8, Paul says his preference is to be at home with God. Home is where we relax and get comfortable. It's the place where we enjoy all the things we love. It's our favorite place to be. We look forward to it at the end of a long day. When heaven is as real to us as it was to Paul, we will long to relax and have meaningful conversation and laughter with God.

Imagine that we get to talk with God face to face! We can ask him questions and hear his voice. And this is my favorite thought about God: The first thing I will see when I open my eyes in heaven after going from this life to the next is God waiting with open arms to give me my first hug and welcome me. Think about God himself hugging you. What a phenomenal thought!

In Matthew 18:10, when Jesus was speaking of the children, he says that "their angels in heaven always see the face of my Father in heaven." It's commonplace for them. Something they get to do on a regular basis. And when I get there, so will I! Think about what a joy it is to regularly see the faces of those we love here on earth—our spouses, children, parents and siblings. We enjoy this blessing, and there's no such thing as too much of it. So just think of what that will be like with God. We will actually see his face whenever we want.

I can plan how he and I will spend the next billion years, or maybe just the first hundred. I will sit at the feet of biblical legends and hear fantastic stories. I'll hug them and sing with them.

Reality

All of these thoughts and images keep heaven very real in my heart. Heaven is why we do what we do here on earth. It should be what motivates us to keep going when things begin to look and feel impossible. If heaven is not real to you, you will have a hard time making it all the way to the end of your trials because there's nothing to work for. It can't be a vague sense of pearly gates and eternal dwelling. It's got to be the details of God's house, his home, impressed upon our hearts...burned into our very souls, and so much so, that, like Paul, we'd rather be there than here: "I desire to depart to be with Christ, which is better by far" (Philippians 1:23).

Just imagine always being at peace, always being happy, always feeling loved, always having hope fulfilled. That's heaven!

Matthew 22:30 tells us that when we get to heaven, in some ways we will be like angels. No more of the burdens that come with being people on this earth. All of that will be forever gone.

We can't allow Satan to cause us to lose heart. If we want to make it to the other side of a trial, we have to fix our eyes on what is unseen: God, his angels, heaven. We have to quit zeroing in on the here and now...the circumstances we are in and the specifics of each incident. Focusing on them doesn't make it any easier. It only depletes us emotionally, leaving us nothing left with which to battle Satan. It is when we are challenged that his real battle for our soul begins.

Remember that what is seen is temporary. It will go away, although it may not feel like it at the time. What is unseen is eternal. This will not go away. We get to have it forever. (See 2 Corinthians 4:18.)

❊

So whatever trials life has served you, remain faithful through them. Our hope cannot be in this life because the time comes for all of us when this life is over. Our comfort as disciples is in knowing that when that time comes, the angels will carry us to the arms of God (Luke 16:22).

Keep the faith!

Epilogue

PARTING THOUGHTS

———

Throughout this book I have shared with you the many ways life can bring about change. Adaptation and surrender are key. These pave the road for God to bless you:

> Endure hardship as discipline; God is treating you as sons.... God disciplines us for our good that we may share in his holiness.... It produces a harvest of righteousness and peace for those who have been trained by it. (Hebrews 12:7, 10)

At This Writing

I wish I had a nice, happy continuation to our life's story to tell you. The truth is, sometimes life just does not get wrapped up with a pretty bow at the end. The past four years have been a continued challenge. We are still in need of help from shelters, food pantries, our family and friends. God has provided tremendously through them. We continue to receive great support from the benevolence committee in our church, for which we are forever grateful. I guess you could say that we are taking life one day at a time. Each day is a new lesson and a different opportunity to grow closer to each other and to God.

As life goes on, difficulties have continued to come our way. Our daughter Briana recently was in a very serious car accident that has left her battling a brain injury. We found out that my father is losing his battle with cancer, and my mother had a health scare that brought her close to death only six weeks ago.

However, we can see God at work even under these circumstances. Our church family has completely embraced our family and taken tender care of Briana. God has used this opportunity to draw my mom closer to him spiritually. Our marriage has deepened and been enriched in ways it may not have otherwise, and our familial bond is stronger than ever.

There are continued bright spots as well. Our son, Travis, is a junior in high school. God has given him many athletic gifts, which he is using to honor him. This year he is the varsity quarterback for his school's football team. This past summer his team beat out forty other teams in the state of Georgia. He was awarded the privilege to represent the Atlanta Falcons in Minnesota for the NFL 7 on 7 Championships. His team took second in the nation. He is working hard to earn a football scholarship to the college of his choice. We are praying he will see his dreams come true. He is also leading a Bible discussion group on his campus and is helping several of his friends to become Christians. He is a great big brother to his two younger siblings. They are both completely enamored with him; in their eyes, he is a hero.

Our youngest son, Elijah, is continuing to develop. We learned this past summer that he has a chromosomal disorder that is the genetic link for mental retardation. Although he will not be able to learn and develop at the same rate as other children, he is in an amazing school with the best teachers and therapists. We could not be more grateful for how God has looked out for him and his very special needs.

Kiara just started kindergarten, and she is loving every minute of it. She is a sponge when it comes to reading and writing. She is already being tested for the gifted and talented program, another kiss from God. I think she can spell words that actually give me difficulty. We can't wait to see where that thirst for knowledge takes her. She is her brother's best friend, and the two of them function like a set of twins.

Bryan graduated with his Master's degree in accounting last year. He was at the top of his class with a GPA of 4.0. With the change in our economy, he is still looking for work and an opportunity to use his degree. As always, he is forever faithful in knowing God will provide the perfect job at just the right time.

I am enjoying watching my children flourish and change. They inspire me daily. It is very special to begin developing an adult friendship with my two older kids. We are at the time in life when you are no longer just parent and child, and this is very exciting. They make me laugh a lot and remind me to have fun. My battle with emotional and physical illness is ongoing, but I do believe I grow a little bit stronger each day. I have no idea what the future holds but with God at the helm, we cannot go wrong.

Thank You, Jacob

I am grateful for Jacob's example. He fought hard at a time when he was most likely tired (at night) and therefore a little vulnerable. God has had to work on my heart quite a bit during difficulty. In my wrestling matches with him, my weaknesses have certainly been revealed. I have learned that my tendency is to quickly give in when I am worn out or sense that I may be easily beaten.

However, if I choose to learn from Jacob, the lesson for me becomes,

> I cannot allow myself the option of sitting down or relaxing at all during the fight. I need to dig deep and not be overpowered by whatever it is I am facing. I need to hang in there until God reveals the blessing...and surely there will be one.

Jacob was left with his hip permanently wrenched. He was forever changed physically, but, more importantly, he was left much stronger spiritually. When I remove the fear of pain from the equation, I allow God to forever strengthen me spiritually. What mark are we allowing God to leave on us? Is it evident to all that we are winning the battle?

I want to be as determined as Jacob was. I need to learn to be as aware of God during the battle as he was. I can't afford to lose perspective because of the level of difficulty I am facing.

The intensity or length of the battle is not what determines whether God is with us. Our feelings may tell us otherwise, but the Scriptures are clear. God says to us as he said to the Israelites: "I will never leave you, nor will I forsake you" (Joshua 1:5). His promise is unconditional and all inclusive.

My heart's desire and prayer is to be willing to accept what lies before me in life, being confident that I am not alone. God's Spirit will always be directing my steps.

The Hawkins Family

Appendix

THE RIDE OF YOUR LIFE

At the end of the annual Super Bowl, the MVP is asked, "What are you going to do now?" He usually smiles and shouts, "I'm going to Disney World!"—the amusement park best known around the world for creating family fun and a lifetime memory. It's where both young and old alike get to be a kid for the day...age has no significance.

Most of us view amusement parks as some of the best places for entertainment. They bring in millions of dollars in revenue annually. We pay someone money to terrorize us on some of these rides and call it thrilling. It excites and scares us all at once. For anywhere from a minute and a half to three minutes, our world spins out of control, throwing us for loops and turning us wrong side up, and we scream and laugh our entire way through it. Once it's over, we run to a different line to get on a different ride that will give us more of the same at different angles. In fact, we spend an entire day with our families at amusement parks in this revelry and actually believe we've had fun when it's all over.

Sometimes, life can be like an amusement park ride. But instead of purposely standing in a line anxiously awaiting our turn at this twisted torture, it seems as if we somehow were accidentally dragged onto the world's most treacherous roller coaster against our will. The metal bar has pinned us in the seat before we have time to voice our objections to even being on the ride. Then we are taken through what feels like the most horrifying twists and turns imaginable.

We're shaken, turned upside down, inside out, racing backward and forward alternately, experiencing full circle flips and speeds that seem unattainable to human beings. All the while, we're dizzy, vomiting, fighting to breathe, beginning to hallucinate and desperately trying to get the attention of the little man who controls the lever to the ride so he can stop it and let us off. But every attempt we make from screaming to flailing our arms and dumping out our pockets on him are all to no avail. He doesn't seem to hear or even notice us. He's looking the opposite direction, unfazed by our panic and near hysteria. We then realize we are not getting off until he says so. We are at his complete mercy—whether that means minutes or hours.

Do you ever feel like your life is like this? It has spun out of control, and you beg and plead with God (the little man with the lever) to stop the ride and let you off, but he does not appear to be listening. No amount of effort on your part is able to stop what is happening to you. If so, consider the one detail in this scenario that is off: The little man with the lever who seems to be ignoring you is not God, but rather Satan. He doesn't care about your pain, panic or hysteria, and he only thinks he controls the lever. The truth of the matter is that God does, of course, and there is a larger plan at

stake: the plan of your entire life and not just the immediate crisis you are in.

You see, when the ride finally does stop, we hope
to never again have that experience. We then turn and
enjoy all the other treats that are fascinating and enjoy-
able in the park: warm pretzels, popcorn, chilidogs, the
show under the big tent and the fireworks. The grand
finale is always spectacular.

By the end of the day, we come home, our arms
loaded down with prizes, balloons and stuffed ani-
mals...and memories that sparkle and shine. In com-
parison to the entire day, that one ride isn't what
stands out in our mind anymore. Our souvenirs
remind us of what was truly special about our adven-
ture. We've got to learn to stick around until the grand
finale and not go home after that first awful ride.

What makes this possible for all of us is our relationship with God, and believe me, his grand finale will
be well worth the wait. No matter how shaky our ride
of life becomes, we can rest assured that God has us
safely buckled in, and he does see and care about our
fear and anxieties. There will also be lots of wonderful
prizes along the way.

Books for Overcomers

Mind Change—*Thomas A. Jones*

Life is full of challenges. Pain. Illness. Persistent sins. Misunderstanding. Insecurity. Disappointment. Abuse. Discouragement. Depression. Failure. Fear. Rejection. Opposition. Confusion. Death. None of these surprise God. He has a plan for us to overcome them all. This book is written to help you see (1) your challenges are not unusual and (2) God's plan for overcoming will work powerfully for you as well as for others. In addition to the usual life obstacles, author Thomas Jones lives daily with the challenge of multiple sclerosis. *Mind Change* grew out of his efforts to find God's power in his weakness and to discover the way to live a productive life of impact in spite of things that could hold him—and all of us—back. Available in audio book also.

Dare to Dream Again—*Jeff Chacon*

Short and simple: life hurts and it is hard to keep on going. If you feel this way, then *Dare to Dream Again* is for you. You will hear God encouraging you and calling your name throughout the pages of this book. Whether you've lost a loved one, lost your health or lost your faith; whether you've been in and out of church leadership, in and out of a job, or in and out of love; whether you've seen a leader fall, seen your child fall or seen yourself fall, the pages of this book will be healing balm for your soul. Through scriptures, songs, original poetry, and an uplifting writing style, you will be helped to recover the quest that God has placed in your heart.

Discover Joy—*Dr. Joy Bodzioch*

Christian psychologist Joy Bodzioch has written this book on finding mental well-being by applying the Beatitudes to your life. Following Jesus' plan for living our lives will help us find meaning and joy. Sharing from her life, her experience as a professional counselor and as a Bible student, Dr. Joy gives an insightful path to finding biblical help for insecurity, depression, negative thinking and other challenges we face in our Christian walk.

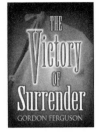

The Victory of Surrender—*Gordon Ferguson*

Surrender equals victory. No paradox is more powerful. No teaching is more needed. No life is more fulfilling. Give up your will to find God's will. And in so doing, find a relationship with God that is full of challenge, yet at the same time, full of peace. Gordon Ferguson explores crucial biblical principles related to surrender, and lavishly illustrates them with stories from his life. His teaching will guide you to "let go" and find real and practical freedom in the sovereign will of God. Includes a study guide for each chapter that helps you to personalize the concepts Gordon is sharing.

Mourning Journey—*Dennis Young*

Minister and grief counselor Dennis Young offers help for all aspects of dealing with difficult times of grief and mourning. He acquaints us with the current under-standings in the field of death and dying. Then he gives us hope and help by interpreting these understandings in the context of Biblical faith. This unique volume addresses a varied audience: the bereaved, those sup-porting the bereaved, the dying, the caregiver, those supporting the caregiver...in short, all of us. Personal

stories of those who have been through the grieving process bring a sense of realness and hope to the book and causes it to reach out to our hearts. More than anything, the author wants us to know that even when life hurts the most, God is still with us and is eager to comfort us.

Rejoice Always—*Drs. Michael and Mary Shapiro*

Two licensed psychologists, who are disciples, unlock some of the mysteries of mental disorders and provide Biblical answers for those seeking spiritual victory. The Bible calls Christians to "rejoice always." For those deal-ing with emotional challenges such as severe depres-sion, bipolar disorder, panic attacks or other psychiatric problems, this message may seem impossible. But with God "all things are possible." In this book you will find (1) a description of various psychiatric problems, (2) causes of such problems, (3) how to evaluate and choose professional help, (4) what to do as a leader working with people with emotional challenges, and (5) most importantly, how a relationship with God enables one to overcome and find the land of "rejoicing."